The
Thingummy

www.**rbooks**.co.uk

The Thingummy

A book about those everyday objects you just can't name

(and the things you think you know about, but don't)

DANNY DANZIGER
& MARK McCRUM

Doubleday

LONDON · TORONTO · SYDNEY · AUCKLAND · JOHANNESBURG

TRANSWORLD PUBLISHERS
61–63 Uxbridge Road, London W5 5SA
A Random House Group Company
www.rbooks.co.uk

First published in Great Britain
in 2008 by Doubleday
an imprint of Transworld Publishers

A CIP catalogue record for this book
is available from the British Library.

ISBN 9780385614566

Addresses for Random House Group Ltd companies outside the UK
can be found at: www.randomhouse.co.uk
The Random House Group Ltd Reg. No. 954009

Typeset in Classical Garamond by Falcon Oast Graphic Art Ltd

Printed and bound in Great Britain by CPI Mackays, Chatham ME5 8TD

2 4 6 8 10 9 7 5 3 1

'Men ought not to investigate things from words, but words from things; for things are not made for the sake of words, but words for things.'

Diogenes Laertius

List of Thingummies

A

Achenes
Aglet
Allen wrench
Andirons
Architrave
Arcuate vanes
At sign @

B

Bain-marie
Beach ball
Besom
Bleed nipple
Bobèche
Bolero
Bolus
Borborygmus
Brannock Device
Burgee
Burpee

C

Cadenza
Calamus
Carabiner
Caruncula
Caryatid
Chiffonier
Clerihew
Contrail
Cradle switch
Crash bar
Croustade
Crozier
Cumulonimbus
Cutwater

D

Dada
Deckle
Deeley-bobber
Desiccant bag
Desire line
Dewclaw
Dibble
Dongle
Dragées
Drupelets

E

Emery board
Emoticon
Escutcheon
Eye

F

F-hole
Farfalle
Fauxhawk
Fines
Fontanelle
Frog

G

Gaff
Gambrel
Garage
Gari
Gasket
Glassine
Gluteal crease
Gnomon
Grawlix
Grubber

H

Hemidemisemi-
  quaver

I

Interrobang

J

Jabot
Julienne

K

Kanji
Keeper
Kerf

L

Labret
Lavaliere
Loupe
Louvre
Lunula

M

MacGuffin
Maxillary central
  incisor
Metonymy
Mirror band
Moonbow
Muffin top
Mule
Muselets

N

Niqaab
Noctilucent

O

Oche

P

Payot
Philtrum
Phloem bundles
Phosphene
Pickguard

Pips
Pistil
Plough
Poof point
Purlicue

Q

Quoin

R

Reredos
Rowel

S

Samara
Shutter release
Soul patch
Sphygmomano-
  meter
Splat
Spogs
Spoiler
Sprocket
Stifle
Styptic pencil

T

Tang
Taupe
Terminator
Tessera
Tines

Tip cup
Tittle
Toast well
Toorie

U

Ullage
Umbel
Umlaut

V

Vibrissae

W

Waldo
Worsted

X

Xbox

Y

Yips

Z

Zarf
Zucchetto

How this book came about

The pair of us were having one of our occasional lunches out. For two professional screen slaves these provide a welcome break from the solitary business of writing. On this particular occasion, at some new gastro pub that Danny had discovered in town, we were halfway through our meal when Danny leaned forward and pointed at Mark's upper lip.

'You've got a splash of gravy on your, er . . .'

Mark dutifully wiped the spot.

'No, not your lip, just above . . .'

'My nose?'

'No, the bit below your nose, above your lip, on your, your . . . thingummy.'

Neither of us, it turned out, knew the word for that intriguing bit of face between the bottom of the nose and the top of the lip. Being mildly obsessive wordsmiths we had to find out. A day later, Danny phoned Mark with the answer, which he'd learned from his doctor friend Rob. Philtrum. John Major has a long one. Adolf Hitler and Charlie Chaplin covered theirs with a moustache. SAS men can, apparently, tap you there in a certain way and kill you. We were both happy to know the right word for this thingummy.

'And Mark,' continued Danny, 'I was just thinking . . .'

And so this book was born. As Danny pointed out, our world is littered with things we ought to know the names for, quite often nearly know the names for, but, at the end of the day, we don't. Thingummies. Thingamajigs. Whatchamacallits. Or if you're American, doohickeys, hoojamaflips or gizmos. Once we started to think about it, there were so many out there.

Now we didn't want to get sidetracked by the many extraordinary and unlikely terms for things that are used by specialists. Surgeons know their **bistoury** from their **snare**, their **endoscope** from their **speculum**, just as steam-engine enthusiasts know their **flywheel** from their **piston rod** and their **slide valve** from their **steam inlet**. But these, we felt, were not strictly thingummies, because no ordinary person is likely to be called upon to use them.

No, thingummies, we decided, had to be those things that we see, touch and use every day. Which are between our fingers and under our noses – and yet we cannot put a name to them.

Many of them are objects. The **dongle** you plug into a computer, the **aglet** at the end of your shoelace. Some are things we barely notice we are using, such as the **runner** on an umbrella. Did you know that was the name for the little bit of metal you push up the **shaft** to hold up the **canopy**? Others are things that we see around us but have never thought to learn the name for: the **labret** piercing on a teenager's lip, the **phloem bundles** of a banana, the **cutwater** on a bridge.

After careful consideration, we decided to add a few entries from a second, more conceptual category, namely those words that lurk at the back of our brains, that we were probably once told or taught, but have now forgotten. **Metonymy**, for example, that figure of speech that most of us use or read an example of every day. Perhaps we kind of know what it means, but could we explain to someone else its precise definition? And what exactly – for those of a more artistic inclination – is **Dada** when it's at home?

As we thrashed out our long list, and then argued our way down to a short list, we realized that, quite often, one person's thingummy is another person's favourite, most familiar object. Most women know the difference between a **kitten heel** and a **court shoe**. But many men don't, and may well go to their graves without ever knowing the correct word for their partner's favourite footwear, let alone who designed it.

It is for people such as this – by which we mean, pretty much everyone, ourselves included – that we've written this little book. It is not intended as a strenuous study course, more as a laidback perusal, perhaps in the bath or the smallest room in the house. Miraculously, this will transform you from someone who is occasionally lost for words, to that far more dynamic person who – obviously in an understated and discreet sort of fashion – always knows the right word for everything.

Along the way you may start to feel some shame that you didn't know this stuff earlier.

Most of us eat three meals a day, with knife, fork and spoon, yet how many of us know what actually spears the food and gets it up into our mouth? The **tines** of a fork, of course. Those seeds that decorate the outside of a strawberry? **Achenes**. There are, on average, two hundred of them per fruit. Once one has the word at one's fingertips it seems inconceivable – and almost sad – that one might have gone through the rest of life without learning it.

As we grow older, of course, more and more things become thingummies. Chefs who once knew their **coquille** from their **cocotte** and their **bain-marie** from their **brochette** will get to a point in life where, even if they can remember the correct word, they can't necessarily be bothered to use it. At that point, the tried and tested line, 'Could you pass me the, that, er . . . thingummy,' becomes all too useful.

Eventually, for some of us, comes that sad moment when pretty much everything is a thingummy – even, perhaps, our nearest and dearest. Before we reach that stage, and in celebration of the wonderful range of terms that exist to describe specific things in our daily life, here is our selection of thingummies.

Achenes

(pronounced a-keens)

are the tiny yellow seeds in a strawberry's skin.
The average strawberry has around 200 achenes.

Actually, botanically speaking, the achenes *are* the fruit; the
strawberry is simply the receptacle into which the fruits are
embedded.

In medieval times strawberries were regarded as an aphrodisiac,
and soup made of strawberries, borage and soured cream
was traditionally served to newlyweds at their wedding
breakfast.

The strawberry as we know it today came about by
chance, after the cross-pollination of two native American
strawberries: the scarlet Virginia strawberry from North
America, and the Chilean strawberry – as large as a walnut,
with a delicate aroma and a pale, almost white flesh. It was
a match made in heaven. The Chilean strawberry gave size
and firmness to the new fruit, while the wild Virginia
strawberry added flavour.

Jean-Baptiste de la Quintinie, the reclusive ex-lawyer
who was gardener to Louis XIV, is credited with being the
first to grow this hybrid in Europe. He was a pioneer of
early cultures, producing lettuce in January and
strawberries in March, as well as introducing such exotic
newcomers as figs and melons to the royal table.

Strawberries contain more vitamin C pound for pound than oranges, and are high in fibre, low in calories, and a good source of both iron and folic acid. Once picked, strawberries don't ripen further, so you should eat them as soon as possible. Make sure, when choosing your berries, to pick out those with a good healthy red colour, and always with their leafy stem – the **calyx** – firmly attached (once this is removed, an enzyme that destroys vitamin C is released). If any of the berries has mould, avoid the punnet; the chances are the spores will have spread throughout.

An *Aglet*

(or aiglet)

is that little plastic or metal tube at the end of your shoelace.

The aglet's purpose is to stop the thread of the lace from unravelling, as well as making it easier to feed through the shoe's eyelets. (The word comes from the Old French *aguillette*, which is the diminutive of *aguille*, meaning needle.)

Aglets go back a long way. Before the invention of plastic, they were made of metals like copper, brass and silver, and even glass and stone. They were often ornamental and some were fashioned into small figures. (In Act I of Shakespeare's *Taming of the Shrew*, Petruchio's servant Grumio talks of marrying him off to 'a puppet or an aglet-baby'.)

Should your aglet break, you may of course just buy another shoelace. But if you're a more frugal kind of person, the aglet can be easily repaired. Shoemakers recommend the following methods:

- ✦ dripping candle wax or resin on to the broken end
- ✦ soaking the lace end with glue or nail polish
- ✦ binding the lace end with fine thread over glue (known as 'whipping')
- ✦ winding adhesive tape round the lace end
- ✦ replacing the broken aglet with heatshrink or small-gauge metal tubing, used respectively by electricians and hobbyists.

Before you tie those laces and walk off, turn your shoe over slowly and consider the other parts for which you may well not know the names. Of course we all know the sole – the bottom of the shoe; and the insole – the interior bottom of the shoe, to which extra insoles may be added, to make the shoe fit tight, or even perhaps just to soak up sweat. But what about the **vamp**, the front of the **upper** of the shoe, crucial in holding the shoe on to the foot. In the case of a sandal or flip-flop (or 'thong' as the Aussies call it), this may be just a couple of leather straps.

The **quarter** is the name for the sides and back part of the shoe; and the **throat** is the central part of the vamp leading down to the **toe box**, **cap**, or **puff**. The top of the shoe, where leather meets sock, is the **topline**; and the **welt** is the ridge that runs along the top of the **outsole**, where it's not covered by the upper.

Men's shoes have two main lacing styles, which relate to their construction. With Oxford style lacing, the eyelet section is part of the quarter, while the **tongue** below is part of the vamp. In the Gibson style, the lacing section is part of the vamp.

GRUMIO: Nay, look you, sir, he tells you flatly what his mind is: Why give him gold enough and marry him to a puppet or an aglet-baby; or an old trot with ne'er a tooth in her head, though she have as many diseases as two and fifty horses: why, nothing comes amiss, so money comes withal.

The Taming of the Shrew, Act I, scene 2

A AGLET

An *Allen wrench*

is an L-shaped six-sided wrench, which can drive a bolt or screw very tightly into a recessed hexagonal socket hole.

It is just one of the very useful tools on the new Wenger Swiss Army Knife, called the Giant Collector's Knife, which has 87 implements.

Aside from two 4 mm Allen wrenches, this bristling behemoth has – to highlight just some of its features – a dozen or so blades, three types of pliers and countless screwdrivers, including a screwdriver specifically for gun sights. It has an implement designed to tighten spikes on a golf shoe. It has saws. It has a reamer, which is a tool to make or enlarge holes, and another tool just for opening the case of a watch. It has a bicycle-chain rivet setter, a signal whistle, cigar-cutting scissors, a laser pointer, a torch, a tyre-tread gauge, magnifiers, a fish descaler, nail clippers and a nail file, plus the requisite toothpick and tweezers. For the avid gardener, there are four different blades for grafting one plant on to another.

It also has a keyring at one end – although you're not likely to lose your keys if this monster is attached. The knife weighs 2 pounds and 11 ounces, and is just under 9 inches wide.

Andirons

are the cast-iron stands on which logs are laid for burning in a fireplace or grate.

Nowadays, they are just as often placed in front of the hearth, and used to prop up tongs and pokers, small shovels and brushes. In the past, andirons were used for cooking, with uprights to hold spits, and attached arms or hobs to keep stewpots and casseroles hot.

Andirons are also sometimes called **fire-dogs**, because during the Middle Ages blacksmiths often made them in the shape of hunting dogs. By the time of Louis XIV (1643–1715) the simple andiron had become elaborately ornate, inlaid with gold and silver, and patterned with fleur-de-lis and heraldic ornaments.

An *Architrave*

is the plain or moulded section above (or around) a window or door. But also – and originally – in classical architecture, architrave is the term for the main beam that rests across the tops of the columns of a temple.

Above the architrave comes the **frieze**, which generally consists of alternating ridged and plain blocks of stone known as **triglyphs** and **metopes**. On top of that is the **cornice**, which completes the **entablature**, as this external upper section of a Greek temple is known. This may in turn be surmounted by a triangular section, the **pediment**, which may include within it sculptural decoration known as the **tympanum**.

The precise structure of the entablature is different in each of the three classical Greek orders of architecture: Doric, Ionic and Corinthian. The proportions of the entablature relate strictly to those of the columns, and vary according to the order. In the Ionic order, for example, the height of

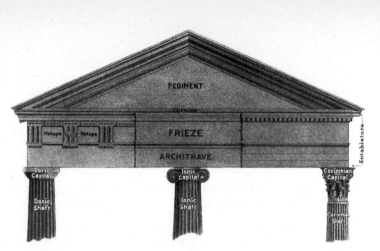

the architrave is half the diameter of the column base; and the dimensions of the rest of the entablature are calculated as fractions of this measurement.

The Doric order came first, invented in the second half of the seventh century BC, possibly in the Greek city of Corinth. Simple, baseless columns rose direct from the raised **stylobate** (floor) up to a spreading **capital** – the convex **echinus** supporting the square **abacus**. The most famous Doric building in the world is the Parthenon.

The more exotic Ionic order evolved at much the same time in the Greek cities of Asia Minor. Columns were taller than Doric ones, with capitals consisting of carved **scrolls**, or **volutes**. They sat on elaborate bases, made up of a square **plinth**, which was surmounted by layers of double roundels and **scotiae** and then the decorated **torus**. Ionic columns also incorporated a new architectural feature called **entasis** – a bulge in the column to make it look straight to the naked eye.

The Corinthian order came later, in the fourth century BC. Now the fluted columns were topped with capitals featuring carved flowers and acanthus leaves below a much smaller scroll, the **helix**.

The Romans used all three of the Greek orders and added two more of their own, the decorative Composite and the simple Tuscan.

These five famous classical orders are not just of interest when wandering around the ancient temples of the Mediterranean. Many of the buildings we see around us today have some classical elements, even if they are not completely **neoclassical**. Look up as you pass along a street. The simplest window may have nothing but a sill, but many are surrounded by architraves and some may be topped by cornices. Following the classical original, a frieze may be introduced, or the cornice may be topped with a pediment. A really elaborate window may feature a full order of **colonettes** rising from a bracketed sill, surmounted by a completely pedimented entablature.

Until the start of the twentieth century, architects generally possessed a familiarity with classical architecture, but this diminished as the Modern Movement became established. Modern architects deliberately avoided classical forms on the grounds that they had become sterile and overused. By the 1950s classicism seemed finished in the UK. Classical solutions to architectural competitions were not taken seriously. Much of the work of the great post-war building boom reflected this lack of interest in neoclassical forms.

But the ugliness and unpopularity of many of these buildings led eventually to a reigniting of the interest in classical forms. In 1992, after a successful series of annual Summer Schools in Civil Architecture, the Prince of Wales established his Institute of Architecture to promote classical and counter-Modernist architectural values. He had earlier dubbed a proposed extension of the National Gallery in Trafalgar Square 'a monstrous carbuncle on the face of a much-loved and elegant friend' and suggested that the rubble left by the Luftwaffe had been less 'offensive' than the architecture of certain contemporary City buildings.

Arcuate vanes

are the concentric raised ridges running around the top of your Frisbee.

Arcuate simply means bowed or arched. After a botched catch, the roughness of the vanes is the cause of that most common and painful of Frisbee sporting injuries – the Frisbee finger. The aerodynamic reason for their presence is that the vanes near the leading edge act as **turbulators**, which force the airflow to become turbulent after it passes over them, which in turn reduces **flow separation** and thus improves the Frisbee's flight.

The Frisbee's origins can be traced back to a bakery – of all things. In 1871, in the wake of the US Civil War, William Russell Frisbie moved to Bridgeport, Connecticut, to manage a branch of the Olds Baking Company of New Haven. He made such a success of the place that he soon bought it outright, and named it the Frisbie Pie Company. Under his direction, and subsequently that of his son, Joseph P. Frisbie, the small company prospered, and grew to an empire of 250 shops. Their most popular items were the Frisbie Pies, which were sold along with their tin baking dishes (a five-cents deposit was refunded if you returned the dish).

Students at nearby Yale then discovered that these baking tins could sail through the air, albeit with a wobbly and unpredictable trajectory, and soon you couldn't walk past a college building without being clocked on the head by one.

Some time in the mid 1940s, a businessman and inventor called Walter Morrison decided to develop the recreational possibilities of these grown-up toys, designing the world's first plastic flying disc, which he called the Whirlo-Way. This he followed in 1955 with a disc which exploited the public's interest in UFOs by looking like a flying saucer – the Pluto Platter.

In 1956, Morrison sold the Platters idea to Ed
Headrick at Wham-O, who improved the aerodynamics of
the discs by building in arcuate vanes. He called his version
Rings of Headrick, but this name didn't catch on. They
were universally known as Frisbees, even though the
original pie company had by then gone out of business.

By the early 1970s, Ultimate Frisbee, a non-contact team game
for two teams of seven people, was being played all over
the world. Today, you can still hardly visit a college
campus, playground, or stretch of beach where you won't
see a Frisbee being tossed around by devoted Frisbyterians.

The *At sign* @

was originally an abbreviation of the phrase 'at the rate of' and was incorporated as a standard key on the earliest typewriter keyboards. Its official typographic nomenclature is **commercial at**.

For a while, in the late twentieth century, when mental arithmetic was being replaced by calculators, and schoolchildren no longer learned how to tally up the price of 30 apples @ 1½*d* an apple, it looked as if the dear old @ sign might die out entirely.

However, a rescue was in the offing. In 1971 an American computer programmer called Ray Tomlinson who was working at BBN Technologies in Cambridge, Massachusetts, on an inter-user mail programme called SNDMSG, sent the world's first email, between two computers which were sitting side by side. Needing to distinguish the name of the user from the name of the computer the user was working at, he decided to reassign the @ sign, so that it now referred to location rather than rate. 'Don't tell anyone,' he is said to have told a colleague to whom he showed his invention. 'This isn't what we're supposed to be working on.' Thirty years later, the use of @ in email is universal.

As most languages didn't use the @ *sign* before the arrival of email, it has earned itself a range of interesting local nicknames. In Polish it is *malpa*, 'monkey', while the Dutch call it *apestaart*, 'monkey's tail'. The Hungarians call it *kukac*, 'maggot', while the Thais are less specific, calling it *'ai tua yiukyiu*, 'the wiggling worm-like character'. In Turkey it's *kulak*, 'ear', and in the Czech Republic *zavináč*, 'rollmop herring'. The Swedes also have a food nickname, *kringla*, 'pretzel', but this is just one of a number of names, ranging from *elefantora*, 'elephant's ear', to *kattsvans*, 'cat's tail'.

A *Bain-marie*

is a double saucepan in which a working liquid, typically water, surrounds sauce or other food which then can be heated more gently and steadily than by naked flame or raw electric element.

Bain-maries are typically used to make such sauces as Hollandaise or *beurre blanc*, which might curdle at a harsher heat. Chocolate sauce, egg custard and lemon curd are also often made in the bain-marie, while oven-cooked dishes such as cheesecake or terrines may be baked sitting in a pan of water to control the temperature – another manifestation of the bain-marie. The word can refer to something as simple as a china bowl sitting over a saucepan of boiling water; and any kind of bain-marie can be used to keep things warm, just as much as for cooking.

The bain-marie is no faddish luxury of the modern world, like the blender or the electric lettuce dryer. Its invention is generally credited to Maria the Jewess (also Maria Hebraea, Maria Prophetissa), a chemist of ancient times,

who some sources say was Miriam, the sister of Moses, and others a Syrian princess, who visited the court of Alexander the Great and learned the art of making gold from Aristotle. Whatever the truth of the legends, she was undeniably a real person, who wrote about the methods and equipment of alchemical operations, several of which required the gentle heat of her double saucepan, to mimic the process by which precious metals were originally formed in the Earth's crust.

Other utensils around the kitchen that are familiar to the chef but not always known to the amateur cook are:

- the **brochette**, the small skewer or spit on which chunks of meat are cooked
- the **mandoline**, the vegetable slicer with the adjustable blade
- the **ramekin**, the small ovenproof dish, in which starters and puddings are often served as individual portions
- the **timbale**, the cup-shaped mould used for rice or exotic cold starters
- the **zester**, the specialized tool which whips off the **zest**, the outer, coloured skin of citrus fruit.

The French, incidentally, use the word as a slang term for a woman with more looks than brains: *une femme au bain-marie* – a woman with a double saucepan for a head.

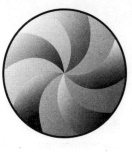

The *Beach ball*

is the multi-coloured, rapidly spinning ball that appears on the screen of Apple computer users when there is a delay in carrying out a command (the equivalent of the egg-timer symbol on a PC).

If the spinning occurs for only a few seconds, this indicates nothing more portentous than visual proof your computer is working hard, that the system is engaged in a processor-intensive activity. But if the beach ball spins for a longer period of time, the situation has morphed into something much more serious. The beach ball's carefree motion is now called **The Spinning Beach Ball of Death (SBBOD)**, and is an indication that all is not well.

Perhaps you are running too many applications at the same time, or there is insufficient free disk space, or limited RAM, or you've just pushed the wrong key. Whatever the problem, invariably the SBBOD spells trouble, and at the very least you are going to have to quit what you're doing – and hope you've backed up the precious work you've been toiling over all morning. You might as well turn off the machine, go and make yourself a cup of coffee, and pray that when you spark up the computer again, you will be SBBOD-free for a decent stretch.

A *Besom*

(*pronounced beez-om*)

is the archetypal witch's broomstick, where a cluster of twigs is tied to a long wooden stick. It was once said that witches disguised their wands as besoms.

In ancient times, besoms were used in every home, and became a symbol of household cleanliness – even though their rounded shape was quite inefficient for sweeping. The Saxons even had 'besom squires', craftsmen who reserved particular coppices where birch and ash for the handles grew profusely. Branches of broom were used to make the sweeping-heads; hence 'broom', a word these besoms came to be known by.

In the early nineteenth century, the Shakers developed the flat broom, which had a far more effective shape for pushing dust and dirt, and immediately caught on. Eventually this put an end to the English besom industry (although Thomas Hardy's *The Return of the Native* (1878) includes a character who becomes a besom-maker).

Because of their association with witchcraft, besoms continued to play a potent part in literature and films. *Fantasia*, for example, the animated Disney film from 1940, has a particularly scary scene – called the Sorcerer's Apprentice – in which Mickey Mouse is terrified by a magic besom, while working for a magician called Yen Sid (Disney spelled backwards).

In the more recent Harry Potter books, magical flying broomsticks are used by players of the game Quidditch. In *Goblet of Fire*, Harry trades up his Nimbus 2000 for a

Firebolt, which is supposed to be the fastest model in the business, as well as the most expensive racing broom in existence.

In *Quidditch Through the Ages*, J. K. Rowling explains that there are three rules of the game that pertain directly to broomsticks:

- ◆ *Blagging*: No player may seize any part of an opponent's broom to slow or hinder the player.
- ◆ *Blatching*: No player may fly with the intent to collide.
- ◆ *Blurting*: No player may lock broom handles with the intent to steer an opponent off course.

The *Bleed nipple*

is the name of the tiny screw that is found at the top end of a radiator and allows the escape of excess air from the system. It sits inside the **bleed valve** and is turned by the **bleed key,** that specialized spanner (usually made of solid brass) that you can never find around the house when you need it.

The bleed valve is not to be confused with the **manual control valve**, which is the one at the top of the little pipe up from the floor that controls the temperature; or the **lockshield valve,** which is the one at the other end of the radiator, having the purpose of keeping the flow of water through the system even.

When new water is added to a central heating system a certain amount of air goes with it. The action of the pump also adds air. This rises in water and collects at high points, preventing the system from dispensing heat properly. If your radiators feel cool at their top ends, you need to bleed them – as follows.

Turn on the heating to get warm water into your system. Then switch it off again. If you keep the pump on, there's always the risk that new air may be drawn in, making your problems worse. Now fit the bleed key into the bleed valve, turn the key anticlockwise half a turn and listen as the trapped air hisses out. Eventually the air will all have gone, to be replaced by first a dribble and then a spurt of dirty water – the **bleed water**.* You should wrap a rag around the key to catch this. A sealed system will now need to be repressurized.

* If the water is brown or orange you have serious problems and should consult a plumber immediately.

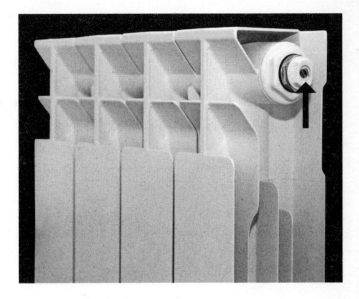

If you should ever get into the disastrous situation where a
jet of boiling water is shooting unstoppably across the
room from the bleed valve, it's highly likely that you have
a) tried to bleed the radiator while the heating was still on,
and/or b) turned the bleed nipple so far in the valve that it
has come loose and shot out on to the floor. Your best bet
in this situation is to jam a towel as quickly as possible
over the leaking valve. Trying not to scald your hands,
then push a knob of Blu-tack into the bleed valve as a
stopgap. Get down on your knees and find the nipple.
Replace it, and screw in tight with the bleed key. Then sit
down, breathe a sigh of relief and vow never to bleed the
radiators with the heating on ever again.

A *Bobèche*

(pronounced boh-besh)

is the ring at the top of a candlestick, used to catch melted wax running down the side of the candle.

This feature was later copied on electric lights. Chandelier bobèches, made from lead crystal or brass, can be much larger than those that would be required by mere candles, up to twelve inches in diameter.

Chandeliers were first used in medieval times to light churches and large halls. The simplest form was a wooden cross, with spikes to hold candles. Subsequently, larger forms of candleholder were devised using ring or crown designs, becoming ever more elaborate. By the eighteenth century, brass chandeliers with curved arms holding many candles were widely used.

As lead crystal became cheaper during the eighteenth century, glass chandeliers became more and more popular. Light was scattered and refracted by the many transparent pendants and chandeliers became beautiful centre-pieces, not to mention status symbols. With the introduction of gas and then electricity, the chandelier continued its magnificent progress, carrying over key features of its candle-bearing days, most particularly the bobèche.

A *Bolero*

is a short jacket usually worn by women. Sleeves may run to the wrist, or be cropped higher up the arm.

Originally worn by matadors in Spain, the bolero is still an essential part of the **traje de luces** or 'suit of lights', the ceremonial gear worn by the **torero** (bull handler) at a bullfight. The silk jacket is often heavily embroidered in gold and can be the handiwork of up to fifty people, costing several thousands of pounds. Beneath are skintight trousers, and on the head a **montera**, or **bicorne** hat. A matador needs at least six such suits a season.

The bolero was also a key part of a woman's wedding dress in nineteenth-century Turkey, where it was twinned with the *salvar* (baggy trousers).

The jazz group Herb Alpert and the Tijuana Brass wore matching bolero jackets in the 1960s and 70s; and the garment found stardom again in the 1990s when Paul Mercurio wore one in the climactic scene of the Australian hit film *Strictly Ballroom*.

In the world of ballroom dancing, a bolero is not as a rule a jacket but a romantic dance, which originated in Spain in the late eighteenth century and subsequently became popular in Cuba and Latin America. It was further popularized across the world when in 1928 the French composer Maurice Ravel wrote his ballet score *Bolero* for dancer Ida Rubenstein, which was a huge hit at its American premiere. The catchy one-movement orchestral piece re-emerged in the late 1970s in the film *10*, which featured Dudley Moore and Bo Derek as a middle-aged songwriter and a gorgeous young bride (not his) who ended up making love on a beach to the insistent ostinato rhythm. Sales of the music subsequently rocketed worldwide, and were repeated in the mid 1980s following the medal-winning ice-dance performance of Jayne Torvill and Christopher Dean.

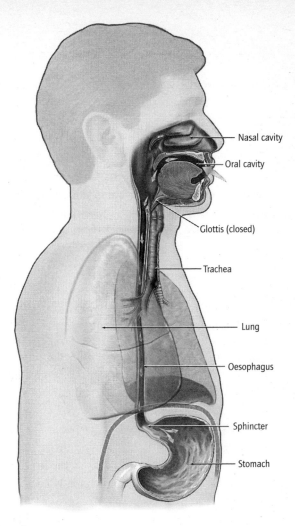

Nasal cavity

Oral cavity

Glottis (closed)

Trachea

Lung

Oesophagus

Sphincter

Stomach

A *Bolus*

is a lump of food, *while* it is actually in your
mouth: a soft, soggy, roundish wad of predigested
mush, moistened by your saliva, shaped by your
tongue, and chewed and ground down by your
molars, until it is sufficiently reduced in size to
slide down the hatch.

Borborygmus

(pronounced bor-buh-rig-mus)

is the name for the rumbling, gurgling, growling sounds made by the stomach. These are caused by the movement of fluids and gases, as food, acids, and digestive juices migrate from the stomach into the upper part of the small intestine, before heading on down the 20-foot-long gastrointestinal tract, propelled by a squeezing action known as **peristalsis.**

The average body makes two gallons of digestive juices a day. The hydrochloric acid in your stomach is so strong it could eat into metal, but a special form of mucus protects your inner linings from this acid along the length of its journey.

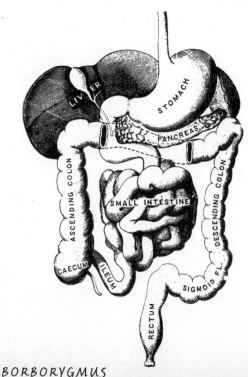

B

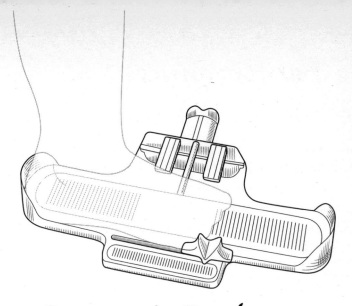

The *Brannock Device*

is that wonderfully old-fashioned-looking measuring instrument, patented in 1926 by Charles F. Brannock of Syracuse, New York, and still found in almost every shoe shop on the high street.

All feet, adults' and children's, can be sized by the same three dimensions that the Brannock Device measures: heel-to-toe, arch (heel to ball of foot), and width.

Slipping your size-four foot into that cold metal was an end-of-holiday ritual, before going back to school and waiting for the next growth spurt.

A *Burgee*

(pronounced bur-jee)

is the little triangular flag that flutters on a sailing dinghy, traditionally at the top of the main mast, but sometimes from a pole on the **bow pulpit** or even in the **starboard rigging**.

As well as giving a useful indication of the direction of the wind, the burgee often proclaims membership of a particular yacht club.

An old tradition dictates that if you visit a club not previously visited by a member of your own, you should exchange burgees. Many yacht clubs display their collections of exchanged burgees – in a case behind the bar, or even, these days, up on a website. Strict etiquette controls the flying of the burgee, as with other maritime flags. It may be flown day or night, but never when racing (when a square racing flag is sported).

As anyone who has been out with a keen dinghy sailor knows, the sport of sailing is littered with precise terms for bits of the boat that it's extremely important to get right. This is not an area where you can get away with 'that thingummy' unless you want to be thrown overboard by your irate captain, whose sense of humour may only return when he (and it so often is a he) gets back to port and into the bar.

A boat is only a boat if it's small; otherwise it's a **ship**. It does not have a left and right, but a **port** and **starboard**; nor a front or back, but a **bow** and a **stern**. The big sail may be the **mainsail**, but the secondary sail is not the lesser or smaller sail, it's the **jib**. The wooden pole under the mainsail is the **boom**. The front of the sail is the **luff** or

leading edge. The taut wires that hold things up are **stays.** Ropes are called **halyards, sheets** or **painters,** unless they hold the sail to the boom, in which case they're **tacks.** The contraption out the back that steers the boat is the **tiller;** the **rudder** is only the bit below the water. Those pincer-like thingummies that hold the sheets in place when you're sailing are **cleats.** That bit of wood that drops through a slit in the centre of the hull is not the thing that holds the boat upright, but the **centreboard** or **daggerboard.**

OK? Now all you have to learn are the terms to do with the actual sailing of the lovely craft. Which, incidentally, is always a female: you sail in her and she speeds over the waves.

A *Burpee*

is a **callisthenic** exercise performed to increase strength and energy; it is named after the American doctor Royal Burpee. The word callisthenic comes from the Greek *kallos*, beauty, and *sthenos*, strength. The burpee is designed to achieve bodily fitness and grace of movement; when repeated, it also improves cardiovascular fitness.

To perform a burpee, move from a standing position to a squat, before thrusting your legs out behind you, while keeping your upper body at arm's length off the ground. The legs are then brought back into a squat, before you spring back to a standing position. For maximum benefit, the exercise should be done in a fluid, constant movement, without pauses.

Much like the Royal Canadian Air Force exercises, the burpee has an institutional following; its devoted adherents range from athletes who have learned it on circuit training to those who have come across it in the services.

A *Cadenza*

is an ornamental passage in a longer piece of music, which allows a soloist to show off their skill on an instrument.

The cadenza originated as a vocal flourish in an opera, when a singer would elaborate on a **cadence** in an **aria** (or operatic song). Later it was taken up in instrumental music, and in due course the improvised element was dropped as composers began writing out their own cadenzas.

Third parties also wrote cadenzas for works by other composers. Beethoven, for example, wrote cadenzas for Mozart's Piano Concerto no. 20; Fritz Kreisler wrote cadenzas for Beethoven's Violin Concerto; and Benjamin Britten wrote a cadenza for Haydn's Cello Concerto in C. In a concerto, cadenzas usually occur towards the end of the first movement.

The tradition was taken up in jazz, and is the right way to describe those bits of the performance where the saxophonist goes off on his own track for a while, to be joined eventually in a funky climax by the rest of the musicians.

The Calamus

is the tube-like part of a bird's feather at its bottom end, where the shaft is hollow and horny, historically known as the **quill**.

When the bird is alive, the word calamus describes the hollow part of the shaft that is embedded in the follicle below the skin. Above the skin the rest of the shaft, which is not at that point hollow, is known as the **rachis**. At the junction of calamus and rachis is a small opening, the **superior umbilicus**, from which often extends a much smaller feather, the **after feather**.

Running outward from the shaft is the **vane** of the feather, consisting of slender filaments known as **barbs**. Attached to these may be further microscopic filaments called **barbules**, which in turn have tiny hooklets, known as **barbicels** or **hamuli**, which hold the barbules together. When you see a bird grooming or preening itself, it's readjusting the lie of its barbules for best insulation and protection against the wet.

The quill is long forgotten now, superseded by the steel nib of a pen, then by the ball of the biro and its followers, and finally by the keyboard of the word-processor. But from the seventh century right up until the early nineteenth century, when steel nibs first appeared, the quill was the writing instrument of choice. Quills were generally made from goose feathers, with the rarer, costlier swan quill for the more discerning or prosperous scribe. Crow-feather quills were said to be excellent for drawing fine lines. The feathers of eagles, owls, hawks and turkeys were also used.

Quills were taken from the left wing of a bird, as those feathers curved outwards and away from a right-handed writer. Only the five outer wing feathers were considered suitable, usually taken from the bird during its spring period of new feather growth.

To sharpen the quill, a special knife was used – the original **pen knife**.

A *Carabiner*

is an oval or D-shaped metal ring with a spring-hinged side that is used by climbers to hold a rope.

Often you will pass someone on a walk in the park with a series of carabiners clipped raffishly to a bandolier around one shoulder – creating a rugged, outdoor look that you've totally failed to achieve in just your tracksuit and trainers.

Carabiners come in two main types: **non-locking** carabiners have a **sprung swinging gate** which can be easily opened to attach a rope or other climbing hardware. **Locking** carabiners have an extra sleeve around the gate, which protects against potentially dangerous accidental opening mid-climb.

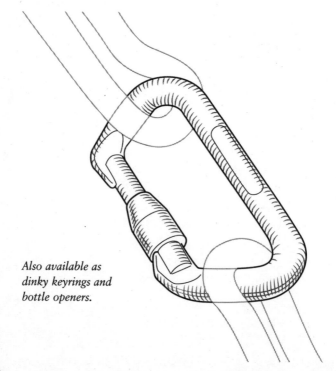

Also available as dinky keyrings and bottle openers.

The Caruncula

is the small, pink protuberance at the corner of the eye.

It is here, after a night's sleep, that a yellowish crust forms, which is a combination of mucus, dust, pollen and tears – **rheum** is the medical term for it, though it's colloquially known as 'sleepy dust' or 'sleep'.

All these substances gather in the eye throughout the day too, but the constant blinking of the eyelids effectively wipes the eyes clean of foreign substances; the secretions only form the crust when the eyelids stop blinking, during sleep.

A *Caryatid*

is a stone carving of a draped female figure, which in classical architecture takes the place of a column or pillar supporting an **entablature** (the upper external section of a temple).*

The word literally means 'woman of Caryae', and one story has it that these stone maidens represent the women of this Peloponnesian town, condemned to slavery because they sided with the Persians during their second invasion of Greece in 480 BC.

The most famous examples are the six figures of the Caryatid porch of the Erechtheum on the Acropolis. Lord Elgin took one of these figures back with him to Britain in the early 1800s; it is now to be found in the British Museum. The other five are in the Acropolis Museum in Athens.

* See **Architrave** (p.19)

CARYATID

Similar figures, but with baskets on their heads, are called **canephores**; they represent the maidens who carried the sacred objects used at the feasts of the goddesses Athena and Artemis.

Caryatids made a reappearance in building façades in the sixteenth century, and can be seen on such disparate buildings as St Pancras New Church, London, the Austrian Parliament in Vienna and the Museum of Science and Industry in Chicago.

    The male equivalent is called an **Atlas**; more than one of these sturdy stone chaps are known as **Atlantes**.

A *Chiffonier*

is a narrow, high chest of drawers or bureau, often with a mirror attached.

Its name comes from the French for 'rag gatherer', suggesting that these pieces were meant perhaps to hold stray household clutter. Many chiffoniers date from the French Empire period (1793–1830) and are often made of rosewood, a timber that was highly fashionable at that time.

Though we spend our days in rooms full of furniture of different varieties, how many of us are truly familiar with the names of these various typical pieces?

- **Armoire** – a tall cupboard with numerous shelves for storage. Armoires are made from a variety of woods: oak, chestnut, mahogany or cherry. Contemporary versions are often used to conceal ugly electronic equipment, such as televisions or computers.
- **Commode** – traditionally a cabinet with one or more doors, generally incorporating a porcelain sink. In English usage, the word has now come to describe a chair that contains a chamber pot. In contemporary French, it's a low cabinet or chest of drawers, usually on legs or short feet.
- **Credenza** – a long, low piece of furniture, generally without legs, containing cupboards, often used as a sideboard or buffet.
- **Danzig chest** – these splendid-looking chests were made from spruce in Danzig, Germany in the sixteenth and early seventeenth centuries. Imported into Britain at this time, they became known as Danzig chests.
- **Escritoire** – a writing desk, sometimes with a hinged top that can be opened outwards to provide a writing surface. Often contains rows of elegant little drawers.

◆ **Ottoman** – an upholstered seat, usually without a back. Often the ottoman is hollow, and may be used as a chest for storing anything from blankets to children's toys.

◆ **Secretary** – a desk with (usually) a base of drawers, above which sits a fold-out desk flap. Above the desk are shelves, often enclosed in a pair of glass doors. A more antique version of the secretary desk may have legs rather than drawers, and just a series of cubbyholes above the desk flap.

◆ **Tallboy** – a tall chest of drawers, often double, with one section standing on top of another. The typical tallboy has five, six, or seven long drawers and two short ones. The earliest seventeenth-century examples are made from walnut; the more common eighteenth-century ones are made from mahogany.

Antique furniture in Britain is generally characterized by the name of the monarch reigning at the time of its design and manufacture. So we move from the sturdy oak constructions of **Tudor Gothic**, the heavy carved work of **Elizabethan**, the lighter ornamentation of **Jacobean**, through the functionality of **Commonwealth**, the lavish Continental designs of **Restoration**, the Dutch influences of **William and Mary**, the developing English style of **Queen Anne**, to the mature splendours of **Georgian**, **Regency** and **Victorian** . . .

Within the Georgian period, a small number of influential designers also gave their names to particularly celebrated styles. So **Chippendale** describes the functional, often heavily carved mahogany furniture designed by the mid-Georgian Thomas Chippendale, and first popularized by his book *The Gentleman and Cabinet-Makers' Directory* (1754). **Hepplewhite** describes furniture manufactured to the designs of George Hepplewhite, detailed in his book *The Cabinetmaker's and Upholsterer's Guide* (1788). Made generally from mahogany or satinwood, these pieces feature more refined carving than Chippendale's. Chair backs are a Hepplewhite speciality, coming in shield, hooped, oval and heart-shaped designs.

Around this time the Scottish architect Robert Adam, who had studied in Italy, brought back the classical lines of Roman and Greek styles to the often huge pieces of furniture that decorated his celebrated interiors, which are noted also for their elaborate **Adam** fireplaces.

The fourth in this golden age of furniture design was Thomas Sheraton, whose book *The Cabinet Maker's and Upholsterer's Drawing Book*, published in four volumes from 1791, set the style for furniture of great grace and delicacy. Sheraton had a special fondness for bureaus and secretaries, often with fancy mechanical parts, featuring inlays rather than carving. He also introduced the roll-top desk.

CHIFFONIER

A *Clerihew*

is a gently satirical, biographical, four-line verse, rhymed as two couplets, often with lines of uneven length. It is named after its inventor, the writer Edmund Clerihew Bentley (1875–1956), who started composing these verses as a boy, when he was bored in the classroom at St Paul's School. He persuaded his friend G. K. Chesterton to write some as well.

Here is one of Bentley's original clerihews from his school period:

> The people of Spain think Cervantes
> Equal to half a dozen Dantes;
> An opinion resented most bitterly
> By the people of Italy.

Here's another:

> Sir Humphry Davy*
> Abominated gravy.
> He lived in the odium
> Of having discovered sodium.

* Whether the distinguished British scientist Sir Humphry Davy
  (1778–1829) really disliked gravy is not known. But the second
  half of the couplet certainly has some truth in it. After the Italian
  scientist Alessandro Volta invented the first battery in 1800, Davy
  used it to isolate sodium and potassium for the first time, and
  later strontium, barium and magnesium, opening up the field of
  electrochemistry. In 1815, after receiving a letter from some
  Newcastle miners which told of the dangers they faced from
  methane gas underground, he invented the Davy lamp, which
  became widely used.

CLERIHEW

A *Contrail*

is the long, thin trail left behind by a jet aeroplane when it's flying high enough for the cold to turn the exhaust vapour into ice crystals. Indeed, a **condensation trail** (to give it its full name) is in effect a very long, thin, man-made cloud.

On rare occasions, you may observe the inverse of a contrail, a **dissipation trail**, where the jet's exhaust appears to cut a slash of clear sky through an already existing cloud. These **distrails** are formed by various effects of the exhaust on the ice particles that make up the cloud.

Contrails may look like big swathes of pollution in the sky, but though they contain hydrocarbons, sulphates, and nitrogen and carbon dioxides as well as water vapour, they produce, comparatively, far less 'greenhouse gas' than motor vehicles or power plants. Modern aircraft engines, which have been designed to burn fuel more efficiently and emit less carbon dioxide, actually create more contrails than their predecessors.

Scientists are still studying the extent to which contrails affect global warming in other ways. It seems clear that, en masse, they create a thin blanket of cloud high up at the top of the troposphere, which has a heat-trapping effect. But it is also true that the highly reflective particles contained in contrails turn back the sun's rays, leading to a global heat reduction.

In the three days after 11 September 2001, when all commercial flights over the US were banned, there were no contrails in American skies, and the difference between daytime and night-time temperatures was found to be 1.1°C greater than normal. The conclusion some meteorologists drew from this was that contrails reduce ground temperatures during the day and increase them at night, which bears out both the effects described above. But the jury is still out on their total contribution to global warming.

Contrails would vanish from our skies overnight if jet aircraft were banned from travelling at high altitude. However, flying lower, aircraft would need more fuel to get through the denser air, with an estimated increase in carbon-dioxide emissions of 4 per cent.

One particular group is totally agreed on the deleterious effect of contrails. Albeit thin, the layer of cloud they create completely spoils the clear skies required by astronomers with land-based telescopes.

'You either give up your cheap trips to Majorca, or you give up astronomy. You can't do both.'

Professor Gerry Gilmore, Cambridge Institute of Astronomy

The Cradle switch

is that part of the telephone on which the receiver-cum-mouthpiece rests.

Even the most contemporary of land-line telephones maintain this feature, though mobiles have dispensed with it entirely. Remember: if you put the receiver down on an outgoing call, the call will be disconnected; on an incoming call, however, the line remains connected until the caller hangs up.

Alexander Graham Bell (1847–1922), the inventor of the telephone, was born into a Scottish family with an enthusiastic interest in communication. His grandfather, Alexander Bell, had been an actor and orator who worked to help people with speech impediments and was nicknamed the 'Professor of Elocution' by the press of his day; his two sons David and Melville followed in his footsteps, becoming elocutionists and speech teachers. Ironically, when Melville married, it was to a deaf woman, Eliza Grace Symonds. Hardly surprisingly, he subsequently became fascinated with ways of communicating with the deaf, developing a system he called Visible Speech Techniques.

As their son, young Alexander, grew up, he attempted to communicate with his mother in his own way: by speaking in a low, deep voice close to her forehead. He remained a curious and inventive child. On a visit to London as a teenager he saw a 'speaking machine' in operation. Inspired, he worked with his brother to develop his own machine, which resembled a human mouth – and which made speech-like sounds. He continued to study the characteristics and patterns of sound, believing that he might eventually find a way to transmit sound electrically. After a bout of tuberculosis killed both his brothers,

Bell moved to North America, eventually teaching Visible
Speech at the Boston School for Deaf Mutes (where he
met and married one of his pupils).

Samuel Morse's development of telegraphy in the
1840s had revolutionized communication, but hand
delivery was still required between the telegraph station
and the recipient. Bell remained convinced that sound
waves, and thus, ultimately, the human voice, could travel
along wires, and he began work on something he called a
'harmonic telegraph'.

He formed a partnership with Thomas Watson,
a scientist who also believed that speech might be
transmitted electrically. On 10 March 1876, while they
were working on their project in separate rooms, Bell spilt
some battery acid over his jacket, and shouted out, 'Mr
Watson, come here. I want you.' A revolutionary moment
had arrived. Watson heard Bell's voice through the wire –
and became the first person in the world to receive a
telephone call.

CRADLE SWITCH

Bell and Watson were able to patent their invention, and became rich. But Bell was never interested in the mere business of telephones, devoting himself instead to other areas of scientific innovation. He contributed to aviation technology and developed a precursor to modern-day air-conditioning in his own home, among other achievements. His last patent, at the age of 75, was for a rapid hydrofoil.

Bell remained committed to the advancement of science and technology. In 1898 he took over the presidency of a small, almost unheard-of scientific society: the National Geographic Society. Bell and his son-in-law, Gilbert Grosvenor, added beautiful photographs and interesting writing to what had been a fairly dry publication – turning *National Geographic* into one of the world's best-known magazines.

Alexander Graham Bell died on 2 August 1922. On the day of his burial, all telephone service in the US was stopped for one minute in his honour.

The *Crash bar*

is the metal bar mounted horizontally across the exit door which you always seem to find at the bottom of echoing stone staircases in theatres and cinemas.

When you push down on the bar, the attached lever forces a latch bolt to rotate and disengage from the **door strike** (the metal plate on the side of the door – or **jamb** – into which the latch fits when the door is closed).

Crash bars may have a retro look, but modern fire codes in countries all over the world require them on all fire and emergency exits.

One of the earliest law codes was the Code of Hammurabi, created in 1760 BC by the Babylonian king of that name. A number of the 282 laws in this code dealt with penalties for shoddy building practices: in particular, if a builder didn't construct a house properly and it collapsed and killed his client, the builder too should be put to death; if the house fell over and killed the son of his client, the son of the builder should be put to death; if it killed one or more of the owner's slaves, the builder was obliged to recompense him, slave for slave.

A *Croustade*

is a moulded or hollowed-out crust, used as an edible serving container for a tasty filling.

Usually made from puff or flaky pastry, croustades may also be fashioned from bread, potato, rice, semolina, vermicelli, or even, in an unusual vegetarian version, chestnuts and pumpkin seeds.

Mini-croustades, filled with such delights as peppered goat's cheese, sun-blush tomatoes, seared sea bass or crayfish tails, are a staple of contemporary canapé menus, alongside many other mini versions of well-known dishes: kebabs, quiches, roulades, and samosas.

Intriguingly, the word canapé derives from *konops*, the Greek for mosquito. From that came *konopeion*, which described an early form of mosquito net, hung over beds. Later the word was assimilated into Old French, where it came to refer to pieces of furniture that incorporated curtains, such as four-poster beds. French chefs took the word from there, to describe a pastry or bread appetizer covered, canopy-like, with a savoury topping.

In the 1970s, when you could still find orange juice served as a starter in neighbourhood bistros, such a thing as a mini-croustade would have been unheard of. At that time the trend-setting hostess's party dishes were full of such tasty morsels as sausage rolls, vol-au-vents, cubes of cheese with pickled onions or wedges of pineapple, and of course the *canapé de résistance*, the devil-on-horseback, a prune (sometimes stuffed with cream cheese) wrapped in bacon.

Inevitably, fashions moved on. At the smart, yuppie gatherings of the 1980s the finger food grew ever more adventurous. Continental treats such as quail's eggs, crostini and bruschette made way in the 1990s for Eastern exotica: Thai fishcakes and chicken satay, Chinese spring rolls, Japanese sushi and nori rolls. As the new century dawned, and the search for novelty grew ever more pressing, mini versions of traditional old favourites began to make an appearance: mini Yorkshire puddings or baked potatoes, caramelized onion tartlets, and of course croustades, cut down and redefined with splendid new fillings.

As tastes turn full circle, one of the seventies favourites has made a reappearance. Championed by chefs such as Heston Blumenthal, the devil-on-horseback rides again – now stuffed with mango chutney and flavoured with a cutting-edge squirt of sherry vinegar.

A *Crozier*

is the long stick – or pastoral staff – carried by a bishop when dressed up in full **vestments** in order to preside at liturgies or confer sacraments. He* bears this to symbolize that he is a shepherd of God's flock.

The traditional curved or hooked top echoes the design of a shepherd's crook and is intended to draw back those who stray, while the pointed **ferrule** at the bottom is there to goad the spiritually lazy. When the bishop is inside his diocese, the staff is held with its curve facing out; when outside, the curve faces in.

Despite its ancient appearance and powerful symbolism, the crozier does not date back to the earliest days of Christianity – it was first used in the Middle Ages. Initially it seems to have been just a straight staff, but a basic bent crook was soon added, which was later combined with designs and figures (snakes and dragons' heads were popular).

* In the UK, bishops are all still male, though since 8 July 2008 the Anglican Church has officially accepted the possibility of female bishops. In the US, the Episcopal Church elected Katharine Jefferts Schori as presiding bishop in June 2006.

The naming of the rest of the bishop's formal gear offers a challenge to all but the most dedicated of worshippers. Starting from the top, the triangular-shaped hat is the **mitre**. The band around the neck is the **amice apparel**, and the little scarf-like bit of cloth that flops down on to the left shoulder is the **lappet**. Below that, the long triangular-bottomed outer wrap is the **chasuble**, decorated on the chest with the highly embroidered band, often of gold, that is the **orphrey**. The scarf that hangs from the left hand is the **maniple**.

On the lower part of the body, below the chasuble, are three layers. The petticoat-like **alb** is covered with the **tunicle** over which hangs the wide-sleeved, loose **dalmatic**. Between the alb and the tunicle hangs the long scarf that is the **stole**.

Below all this, on his feet, the bishop wears **sanctuary slippers**. On his hands he may wear gloves, beneath which will be the **episcopal ring**.

Unlike the parvenu crozier, most of this splendid array of garments can be traced back to the earliest days of the Church. The alb is very similar to the light tunic worn by clergy on a daily basis in those times; the stole is developed from the scarf commonly worn around the neck by the Romans; the chasuble relates back to a simple mantle worn by working people; while the dalmatic was worn by the upper classes in Dalmatia.

Much of the gear is also symbolic: the alb stands for purity and innocence; the stole for patience; and the maniple for strength and endurance.

Cumulonimbus

is the name for that mighty, rain-bearing cloud which resembles a sky-borne mountainous landscape.

Such a cloud can tower up from just above ground level to heights of 45,000 feet, its often dark top spreading out into the freezing upper troposphere as the anvil-shaped **incus** (known colloquially as the 'anvil head'). As it masses up on a sunny summer's afternoon you know that it's time to pack away the beach towels and head for home; this monster signals rain, if not a drenching thunderstorm.

The names for all the main cloud forms come from combinations of five Latin words: *cirrus*, meaning a curl of hair; *cumulus*, a heap; *stratus*, a layer; *altus*, high; and *nimbus*, raincloud. These terms were first suggested in 1802 by the amateur English meteorologist Luke Howard, in a paper to the Askesian Society (a debating club for scientific thinkers which lasted from 1796 to 1807).

Cirrus clouds are found at the highest levels, above 23,000 feet, where temperatures are so low that the clouds are made up of ice crystals. Like the hair they were named after, cirrus clouds often come in isolated tufts, thin filaments, or threads spreading out into featherlike forms. **Cirrostratus**, on the other hand, is a thin, whitish sheet of cloud, sometimes covering the sky completely, often forming a glowing halo round sun or moon. **Cirrocumulus** describes the third kind of high cloud: the beautiful masses of tiny, globular cloudlets sometimes called a 'mackerel sky'.

Between 23,000 feet and 7,000 feet are found intermediate-level clouds with the alto prefix: **altocumulus** clouds may be arranged in groups or lines, often so closely packed that their edges are confused; blue sky can generally be seen behind. **Altostratus,** by contrast, forms a thick grey or bluish-coloured sheet (when it displays a rippling effect it is known as **altostratus undulatus**).

Lower clouds are found below 7,000 feet. The correct name for the famous 'cotton-wool' cloud is **fair-weather cumulus,** so called because it presages a fine day of sunny spells. When the weather starts to turn, the sky fills with the large masses or rolls of cloud known as **stratocumulus,** leaving just the odd patch of blue here and there. These may then be replaced by the mighty cumulonimbus.

The dreary, grey, rain-bearing sheet of cloud which makes a misery of many an English day is **nimbostratus**. This can reach from as low as 1,000 feet up to 20,000 feet. It is not, however, to be confused with the lowest cloud of all, the grey, featureless, but generally dry **stratus**, which may come right down to the ground and also be called **fog**.

 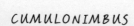

The type of cloud formation present gives an indication of the sort of weather to be expected:

- ◆ Cirrus – unsettled weather coming
- ◆ Cirrostratus – showers or rain soon
- ◆ Cirrocumulus – unsettled weather
- ◆ Altocumulus – sunny periods
- ◆ Altostratus – rain likely
- ◆ Fair-weather cumulus – sunny spells
- ◆ Stratocumulus – dry but dull weather
- ◆ Cumulonimbus – heavy rain or thunderstorm in the offing
- ◆ Nimbostratus – in fact it's raining now

'Clouds are subject to certain distinct modifications, produced by the general causes which affect all the variations of the atmosphere; they are commonly as good visible indicators of the operation of these causes, as is the countenance of the state of a person's mind or body.'

Luke Howard, 1802, in a paper to the Askesian Society

The *Cutwater*

is the triangular stone part of a multiple-arch bridge, between the arches, that breaks (or cuts) the water flowing past.

The arches themselves are mounted on the **piers** of the bridge, which are hidden beneath the water. The point at which the piers meet the arches, around the water-level, is called the **springing**. At each end of the bridge you find the **abutment**, which restrains the horizontal thrust of the bridge and its load.

The width of each arch is described as its **span**; the height as its **rise**; and the relation between these two measurements is known as the **span-to-rise ratio**. Florence's famous Ponte Vecchio, which was built in 1345 after the destruction by flood of its wooden predecessor, is an early example of a high span-to-rise ratio, namely 5:1. Arch bridges were first used by the Romans, though the stone arch itself was a feature of the Indus Valley civilization of 2500 BC.

Dada

refers to an artistic movement that flourished between 1915 and 1923 and is important for its huge influence on the art of the late twentieth and early twenty-first centuries.

Dada evolved during and immediately after the First World War, mainly as a response to the huge death toll of that appalling conflict. It started in the neutral city of Zurich, spread to Barcelona and New York, then after the war to Berlin, Cologne and Paris. The Dadaists were opposed to the so-called 'rational' forces of science and technology which had, as they saw it, brought civilization to its knees. Their artistic response – which some called 'anti-art' – was deliberately absurd, confrontational and nihilistic. But this wasn't a movement of arty conscientious objectors or pacifists. Many of the key figures in Dada – such as Otto Dix, George Grosz and John Heartfield – had enlisted and fought.

It's not known exactly when the name Dada was first coined or why. Perhaps it was a deliberately nonsensical word, for a movement that mocked sense. Or it originated from the French word *dada*, which means a child's hobby-horse. Or it came from the Slavic words for 'yes, yes', as used by Romanian Dadaists Tristan Tzara and Marcel Janco. Or the original Zurich group came up with it by jabbing a dictionary at random with a paperknife. All these stories have been suggested. But true Dadaists in any case would have spurned the use of a name for their movement, or indeed the idea that their nihilistic work was a movement at all.

In the long term, the most influential of the artists known as Dadaists was perhaps Marcel Duchamp, who came up with a series of works he called 'readymades'. The most famous of these was *Fountain*, a urinal signed on its rim in capitals with the pseudonym R. Mutt and submitted to the annual exhibition of the Society of Independent Artists in New York in 1917. Unsurprisingly, given the prevailing propriety of the period, it was rejected.

Though largely unappreciated at the time, such work foreshadowed and made possible **conceptual art**, art in which the idea, rather than the object itself, is paramount. As the twentieth century progressed, similar work continued to be produced, often with a deliberate anti-art flavour.

In 1953 the American Abstract Expressionist Robert Rauschenberg exhibited *Erased De Kooning Drawing*, a drawing by Willem De Kooning which Rauschenberg had rubbed out, raising the sorts of questions that would become all too common later in the century: Is erasing

DADA

another artist's artwork art? If so, is that only because a famous artist like Rauschenberg did it? And so on.

In 1957, the French artist Yves Klein exhibited an empty room, which he called *The Surfaces and Volumes of Invisible Pictorial Sensibility*. As if that hadn't taken things far enough, three years later he jumped out of a first-floor window into the street, an act which he photographed, but which was *in itself* an artwork called *Saut Dans Le Vide* (A Leap Into The Void). 'The painter,' he told his admirers and critics, 'has only to create one masterpiece. Himself, constantly.'

In 1961, the Italian Piero Manzoni defecated into ninety small cans, on to which he wrote 'Artist's Shit'. These he exhibited, putting them on sale for the price of their weight in gold. Later he sold his breath ('Bodies of Air') and signed people's bodies, declaring them to be works of art.

In the summer of 1962 the Bulgarian-born Christo (Javacheff) blocked off a Paris street with a load of oil barrels, creating a huge traffic jam. This work he called *Rideau de Fer* (Iron Curtain). The art, he made clear, was not the barricade, but the traffic jam. It was not the last the world would see of Christo, who together with his wife Jeanne-Claude created many more spectacular **installations**, including the swathing of New York's Central Park in orange banners and the wrapping of eleven islands off Miami in pink polypropylene.

In 1965, the English artist John Latham devised a conceptual art piece called *Still and Chew*. He invited students at St Martin's School of Art (where he himself taught part-time) to chew pages of the influential critic Clement Greenberg's seminal work *Art and Culture*. He then dissolved the results in acid and returned them to the library in a bottle.

Latham lost his job, but conceptual art went from strength to strength. In the 1970s the movement reached a wider audience through two major New York exhibitions, the Museum of Modern Art's 'Information' and the Jewish Museum's 'Software'. By the 1990s, when it was taken up by the Young British Artists, celebrated by the Turner Prize and made notorious by the tabloids, conceptual art had become altogether the fashionable thing. The 1997 exhibition 'Sensation' at the Royal Academy in London sealed its triumphant progress. Since then conceptual works by artists such as Damien Hirst (sharks in formaldehyde), Tracey Emin (unmade bed) and the brothers Jake and Dinos Chapman (mannequins with genitalia instead of faces) are at the centre of a thriving contemporary art market, the blatant commercialism of which would surely have been frowned on by the original Dadaists.

In 2004 a panel of five hundred 'art experts' voted Duchamp's *Fountain* 'the most influential modern art work of all time'.

'The Dada philosophy is the sickest, most paralyzing and most destructive thing that has ever originated from the brain of man.'

The *American Art Review*

The *Deckle*

is that little extra bit of fat which comes with the **point cut** of a **brisket**.

The point cut is harder to find than the more common **flat cut,** which is both leaner and thinner. However, the fat from the deckle greatly improves the flavour of the brisket, if allowed to soak into the meat during cooking.

The brisket itself is the cut of meat that comes from the breast or lower chest of an animal, beneath the first five ribs, behind the **foreshank**. Though all meat animals have a brisket, the term is usually applied to beef or veal. One of the tougher cuts of meat, the brisket needs long and slow cooking to break down the collagen in the connective muscle tissues found in this section of the animal. The meat is often used, chopped, in a pot roast or casserole, or else marinated or smoked. The brisket is a staple of Jewish cooking, often served sliced as an entrée, particularly on religious holidays. Sweet brisket is served at Rosh Hashanah (Jewish New Year) for a sweet new year.

The brisket is one of fourteen **primal cuts** of British beef. The others being, from front to back: **neck and clod, chuck and blade, fore rib, thick rib, thin rib, shin, sirloin, flank, rump, silverside, topside, thick flank,** and **leg.**

Neck and clod is most commonly used for hamburgers and sausages. The rib cuts provide spare ribs and rib-eye steaks. Sirloin and rump are the tenderest and most prized, lending their names to steaks on the table.

A *Deeley-bobber*

is a bizarre party accessory that makes the wearer look (supposedly) like an alien. An Alice band, two glitter balls, or furry ears, perched upon springy 'antlers' – et voilà!

Nothing says party (like it's 1982) more than this wonderful piece of festive gear. In the Deeley-bobber's heyday, no self-respecting fun-lover, male or female, would hit the party without one.

Said to have originated from John Belushi's 'Killer Bees' skit on the famous American TV show *Saturday Night Live*, Deeley-bobbers became popular at a time when aliens were all the rage (and the electronic game of Space Invaders was to be found in every pub in the land). When registering its trademark name in 1982, Ace Novelty Company called it 'a headband with springs carrying ornaments'.

The Deeley-bobber is less often seen now, though it's still a popular accessory at children's parties and hen nights.

A *Desiccant bag*

is one of those bags full of powder you find sometimes in packets and containers.

Its purpose is to bring on or maintain a state of dryness in a product that might be sensitive to moisture or humidity. Two of the most common desiccants are silica gel and calcium chloride. Sometimes you may see more primitive, old-fashioned desiccants, such as grains of rice in salt shakers.

Double-glazed windows also make use of dessicants, which are placed inside the spacer bar between the two panes of a unit to dry out any trapped moisture.

The *Desire line*

is the path that people most want to take, and will take – no matter where an existing track, pavement or road may lead. You can see the desire line, straight or slightly crooked, beaten across muddy fields or grassy hillsides, avoiding the carefully signed route the authorities would prefer you to use.

There are about 146,600 kilometres of public footpaths in England and Wales – in Scotland there has long been a general presumption of access to all land, unless there is a very good reason for the public to be excluded (areas such as quarries, airfields and Ministry of Defence land).

 DESIRE LINE

A path or track that anyone has the legal right to use on foot, and sometimes with other forms of transport, is a **right of way**. Currently these consist of:

◆ **Public footpaths** – open only to walkers (146,600 km).
◆ **Public bridleways** – open to walkers, horse-riders and pedal cyclists (32,400 km).
◆ **Restricted byways** – open to walkers, horse-riders, and riders of non-mechanically propelled vehicles, such as horse-drawn carriages and pedal cycles (6,000 km).
◆ **Byways Open to All Traffic (BOATs)** – open to all classes of traffic including cars, but used mainly by walkers and horse-riders (3,700 km).

County councils are required to produce a definitive map and statement showing the rights of way that exist in their area. They have a duty to keep these maps up to date.

The Dewclaw

is the tiny fifth claw on the inner part of a dog's leg above the other toes, so called, rather romantically, because it brushes the dew from the grass. Dogs almost always have these extra talons on the inside of their front legs and sometimes also on their hind legs.

Some owners and vets say that dewclaws are useless, and should be removed, as they can get torn or cause damage (to clothes, furniture and the like). Others claim that this odd appendage is very useful to a dog: to help pick up bones and sticks; for grip in hunting and climbing; to scratch an itch; even to remove objects stuck in their teeth.

The dewclaw on the front leg is sometimes also described as a **first digit**; in this case, the word dewclaw is used to describe the **vestigial claw** on the rear leg, which is higher up, has no muscular control and, it seems, no purpose.

A number of mountain shepherding breeds – the Saint Bernard, Pyrenean Mastiff and so on – have been selectively bred for **polydactyly** (having multiple digits that are often mobile and controllable).  To meet the breed standards recognized by international Kennel Clubs, dogs must have their fore and/or hind dewclaws intact. Indeed, some double-dewclawed dogs will be favoured over single-clawed equivalents. Many French Beauceron breeders, for example, believe that a dog is not a Beauceron unless it has hind double dewclaws; these enable it to climb on to sheep when herding, as well as helping it move swiftly through snow. The Norwegian Lundehund, likewise, uses its multiple dewclaws to scale cliffs and hunt puffins.

There are many other specialized terms for the body parts of Man's best friend, which anyone wanting to join in those doggy conversations in the park should master. Most would know the **tail, muzzle** and possibly the **hock**, which is the correct word for the joint between the knee and the foot. But how many non-petlovers could place the **croup**, the **withers** and the **pastern**? Those jowly flaps of loose skin round the neck are **dewlaps**; and that red membrane inside the lower eyelid, which you may notice as a dog looks balefully at you while you're eating, is the **haw**.

There are over two hundred breeds of dog and these are split into seven groups,* according to their proportions and characteristics: **terrier, working, gun dog, hound, pastoral, toy,** and **utility**.

◆ Terriers have been bred to flush out prey such as foxes, badgers and rabbits, so are consequently small, to fit into tunnels. They are much more aggressive than their size might suggest. Some breeds are wire-haired to give them extra protection (e.g. Airedale, Norfolk and Scottish Terriers).

◆ Working dogs have been bred to herd livestock, pull sledges, search and rescue, guard or even to identify items such as drugs; they are generally even-tempered, energetic, easy to train and obedient (e.g. Boxer, Great Dane, St Bernard).

* The Kennel Club UK recognizes 209 breeds, The American Kennel Club 148; both have seven groups, although some terms differ.

◆ Gun dogs are bred to have exaggerated instincts and need little training to point or retrieve. **Pointers** (as their name suggests) will spot game and silently point to its whereabouts with raised nose and forepaw, while **retrievers** will retrieve shot game without damage (e.g. Irish Setter, Golden Retriever, Cocker Spaniel).

◆ Hounds have been bred for hunting and tracking. They have an acute sense of smell and will bay when on the trail of a prey. They are renowned for their stamina (e.g. Beagle, Whippet, Greyhound).

◆ Toy dogs are bred for domestic use. They are small and sociable, so are suitable for confined living spaces. Many of the dogs you see trotting round the park after fashionably dressed people in cities are toy dogs (e.g. King Charles Spaniel, Pekinese).

◆ Utility or non-sporting dogs include medium to large purebreds that differ in conformation and characteristics. Some of the oldest documented breeds in the world fall into this category (e.g. Bulldog, Dalmatian, Poodle).

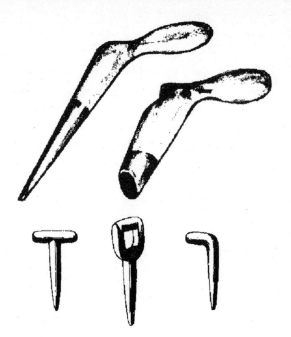

A *Dibble*

(or dibber)

is a pointed gardening instrument used to make holes in the ground, generally for planting bulbs or pricking out seedlings. To dibble is to use such a tool.

When using your dibble to plant bulbs, remember that they should be put in at a depth at least two to three times their height and two-bulb widths apart. When the soil is replaced on top, there should be no air spaces around the bulbs. Spring bulbs should ideally be planted by the end of September, and certainly well before the first frosts set in.

A *Dongle*

is a small **hardware device** that plugs in to a computer, generally to authenticate a particular piece of **software**.

Without the dongle, the software will not run properly, so it can be used as protection against unlicensed copying by unscrupulous users. Generally dongles are attached to expensive, specialized packages such as translation memory or printing software. The dongle may be encoded with a licence key, specific to a particular user, which enables only certain features in the application.

The word dongle has now become general, referring to other computer **plug-ins** such as those that enable Bluetooth, or USB modems which allow you, for a fee, to access Broadband from anywhere with mobile reception.

  DONGLE

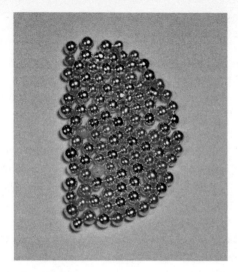

Dragées

(pronounced drah-zhay)

are what discriminating children demand on their birthday cakes.

Otherwise known as 'those little silver balls', they're smaller than a cultured pearl, made of sugar, and covered with a metallic coating to resemble a ball bearing. Generally, they are as tough to crunch through as a real ball bearing. You can also get them with gold and copper finishes.

Sugared almonds are also called dragées. In France and Italy, these are served at wedding parties – traditionally thrown at the newly wed couple – a custom that is supposed to ensure fertility and lifelong prosperity.

Drupelets

are the little globules that make up a raspberry
or blackberry.

Though both fruits are from the same family, raspberry
drupelets are hairy and blackberry drupelets are smooth.
All the drupelets are attached to the central core of the
fruit, which is called the **receptacle**.

One of the most intriguing things about the raspberry is the
word itself – with its curious silent 'p' (also found in
cupboard and psychiatrist). 'C' can be silent too – as in
blancmange and the sceond 'c' in Connecticut – and gnus
and gnats will tell you on no account to pronounce the 'g'
– otherwise they might gnash their teeth at you.

An Emery board

is a strip of cardboard coated with powdered emery used to file finger- and toenails.

Emery comes from corundum, which, after diamond, is the hardest mineral on Earth, as defined by the Mohs Scale of Mineral Hardness, which classifies ten key minerals according to their ability to scratch each other:

Mohs Scale	Mineral	Absolute Hardness (Measured by Sclerometer)
1	Talc	1
2	Gypsum	2
3	Calcite	9
4	Fluorite	21
5	Apatite	48
6	Orthoclase	72
7	Quartz	100
8	Topaz	200
9	Corundum	400
10	Diamond	1500

So if a mineral can be scratched by topaz, say, but not by quartz, then its Mohs hardness is between 7 and 8. Window glass has a hardness of around 6 on the Mohs Scale; a fingernail around 2.5.

Emoticon

is short for **emotional icon,** and is the word for the symbols expressed through the keyboard of a computer or mobile phone to represent human emotions.

:-) is perhaps the most common emoticon, describing a smiling face.

;-) incorporates a wink in one of the eyes.

<|:-) shows someone wearing a hat.

(-_-) indicates a bored face.

:-D is a laugh.

:-@ suggests a scream.

The first and most famous emoticon of all was the Smiley, created in 1963 by commercial artist Harvey Ball as an image for a 'smile campaign' initiated by the State Mutual Life Assurance Company of Worcester, Massachusetts, in an attempt to get their employees to be friendlier as they dealt with customers.

Only a hundred buttons were originally ordered, but the design proved hugely popular; a second order for the buttons was for 10,000. In 1967 a bank in Seattle used the Smiley, which still had no trademark attached, for a marketing campaign and 150,000 buttons were distributed. In the happy, hippy era of the late 1960s the symbol spread across America and the world – more than 50 million Smiley Face buttons were eventually sold.

In the late 1980s, the Smiley symbol had a resurgence, associated in the minds of many young people with ecstasy, raves and acid house music. It also became the subject of a copyright dispute, between the American company Wal-Mart, who were using it to promote low prices, and the Frenchman Franklin Loufrani, who owned a company called Smiley World, and claimed he had created it. Fortunately neither won the right to claim Harvey's happy face as theirs, though Wal-Mart tried – and lost – again in 2008.

As for Harvey Ball, he never applied for a trademark of the Smiley, and earned just $45 for his work. But Mr Ball lived up to the spirit of his design. He remained in Worcester, and his local paper reported him as saying: 'Hey, I can only eat one steak at a time, drive one car at a time.'

E EMOTICON

The *Escutcheon*

is the back plate around a light switch, a door handle or a keyhole.

Escutcheons are both ornamental, in that they draw the eye to the keyhole, and protective, because they safeguard a door's woodwork from marks made by fumbling key-holders, or smudges of dirty fingers around light switches.

Another important item of door furniture is the **finger-plate**. Again, it protects a door from the accumulation of dirt left by people pushing it open with their hand. It is usually positioned at chest height opposite the hinge, which is the natural place to push a door.

An *Eye*

is the name given to any one of the holes in the famous Swiss cheese called Emmental.

The best of this tasty hard cheese, much used in sandwiches and for cheese on toast, is called Emmentaler Swiss. Under European law only cheese made in the Emme valley outside Berne, and by a particular process, may qualify for this label; like a fine wine, it has an Appellation of Controlled Origin.

The milk used to make Emmentaler Swiss should strictly come from pasture-fed cows. When the milk is heated, and various bacteria introduced, bubbles of carbon dioxide form, which produce the holes. Traditionally, the eyes must be between the diameter of a twenty-centime piece, at 21 mm roughly the width of a cherry, and a two-franc piece, which is 27.5 mm across, about the size of a large hazelnut.

There is currently controversy in the cheese world, because the US Department of Agriculture is demanding that the eyes become smaller. This is because American slicing machines are unable to cut cheese with large eyes into thin slices without it crumbling. So the Swiss have been instructed that the eyes must measure between a third to three-quarters of an inch in diameter. The Swiss don't like to be told how to make their cheese, and certainly not by a nation whose only well-known contribution to the art is Philadelphia cream cheese.

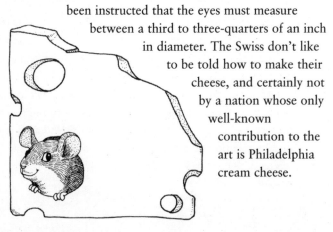

The F-hole

is the long, narrow hole in the **soundboard** (or top surface) of a violin; shaped like an old-fashioned 'f', or 's' to modern eyes, each instrument has two, one to each side of the **bridge**, at the delicate central curve of the **waist**.

The purpose of the f-hole is not merely decorative; it helps the violin project its sound more efficiently; not so much because it is a hole, but because it lets the soundboard vibrate more strongly.

On other acoustic stringed instruments similar sound-holes have different shapes: guitars have circles, lutes have rosettes.

The violin in its present form emerged in the sixteenth century in northern Italy, most likely a descendant of the two-stringed Arabian **rabab** and similar fiddles of Central Asia.

The first violin documented as having four strings was made in 1555 by Andrea Amati of Cremona. Over the next century the instrument gained popularity – by 1660 the French king Charles IX had ordered twenty-four. The Amati family continued to be known for their violin-making. Andrea was succeeded by Antonio, Hieronymus, Nicolo and Hieronymus II. Other celebrated families of **luthiers** were the Guarneri, the Stradivari and the Gagliani. Instruments made by these craftsmen continue to be highly sought-after, by collectors and performers alike. In May 2006, a violin made by Antonio Stradivari (*c.*1644–1737), known as 'The Hammer', was sold at Christie's auction house for the record sum of $3,544,000.

F-HOLE

Farfalle

are the butterfly-shaped pieces of pasta which mix
so harmoniously with tomato or creamy sauces.

You can practically become fluent in Italian by learning the
meanings of all the 600 words for different types of pasta
– which itself means dough.

OK, let's speak pasta:

Anellini	little rings
Cannelloni	big pipes
Capelli d'angelo	angel's hair
Conchiglie	shells
Fusilli	spindles
Lasagne	sheets
Orecchiette	little ears
Penne	pen points
Riccioline	little curls
Rigatoni	derived from the Italian word *riga*, meaning line
Spaghetti	little strings
Stelle	stars
Tripolini	little bow ties
Vermicelli	little worms

You can eat your pasta when it is firm to the bite, **al dente,** or very tender, **stracotta** (which literally means extra-cooked). Some like their pasta very firm, and the term for this is **fil di ferro,** which means wire. You can choose your pasta freshly made with eggs, **pasta all'uovo,** or dry, **pasta secca.** In the region of Emilia-Romagna they colour their pasta with spinach puree, which turns it green, **tagliatelle verde.**

The Fauxhawk

is the hairstyle in which a strip of hair across the top of the head is longer and higher than the hair on the remainder of the head, as worn by David Beckham.

The name is a play on words, referring to the style's more dramatic inspiration, the **Mohawk**, in which the sides of the head are completely shaved, elevating the remaining top hairs to a splendid peacock crest. Often Mohawks are dyed brilliant colours for extra effect. In the UK this style is known as the **Mohican**.

The name comes from the Mohawk tribe of Native Americans, although the style – originally known as the **roach** – was one of several worn by warriors from the eastern Iroquois and Lenape tribes. American Paratroopers of the Second World War adopted the cut, and in the late 1970s it re-emerged in London as part of punk subculture. In the US, it was popularized further by the remarkable Mr T, the actor who played Sergeant Bosco 'B.A.' (Bad Attitude) Baracus in the 1980s television series *The A-Team*.

Another, less common style is the **reverse Mohawk,** where a
line is shaved from the forehead to the nape of the neck,
leaving hair to both sides; this is also known as the
Antihawk, the Skunk, the Highway and the Nohawk.
For those who like the style, but can't quite muster the
commitment, there's always the **wighawk,** a strap-on
version worn by the pop-cyberpunk band Sigue Sigue
Sputnik. There's no need to be ashamed of this accessory,
as Native Americans themselves often wore artificial
roaches, made from the hair of porcupines and the tail
of the white-tail deer.

The **scalplock,** another popular style for Native
American warriors, where a single lock of hair sprouts
from an otherwise bald head, is also traditional among
Ukrainian Cossacks, where it's known as the **khokhol.**
Indeed, 'khokhol' is a common term of abuse amongst
Russians for Ukrainians.

Fines

are the dusty remnants at the bottom of cereal
boxes – particularly delicious in the more sugary
brands.

However, now that artificially sweetened cereals have
been identified as major contributors to children's obesity,
manufacturers are decreasing the amount of sugar added.
(Until quite recently, many cereal brands contained over
55 per cent sugar.)

The cold cereal business began in the late nineteenth century
with the search for a healthier diet, as an alternative to
the heavy meat-laden breakfasts people were eating at
the time, which were causing a variety of gastrointestinal
disorders. In 1863, American James Caleb Jackson
developed the first breakfast cereal, which he called
Granula. It was a healthy concoction of grains, nuts, and

husks of bran. Unfortunately, Granula had to be soaked in cold water at least overnight, and even then it had a rough, tough consistency, felt heavy in the stomach, and by all accounts didn't taste very nice. It was not a commercial success.

Thirty years later, the production of corn flakes began by accident. In 1894, Dr John Harvey Kellogg, and his brother Will, who ran a health spa/sanitarium in Battle Creek, Michigan, were experimenting with new recipes for the vegetarian diet they fed their patients. One evening they left some cooked wheat to rest and when they returned some time later, found it had gone stale. They decided not to waste it by throwing it away, but to process it by pressing it between rollers. They expected to see flat sheets of dough, but instead found flakes, which – economical as ever – they agreed to toast and serve to their patients, with milk.

A year later they filed a patent for 'Flaked Cereals and Process of Preparing Same' which was issued on 14 April 1896, under the name Granose. These eventually became Kellogg's Corn Flakes. After three years, they had sold one million packets.

A *Fontanelle*

is a patch of soft membrane on a baby's head, which has not yet developed into bone; if you look closely, you can see it pulsating.

Though the **anterior** fontanelle at the front is the largest and most visible, a baby has several fontanelles. The next most obvious is the **posterior** – or **occipital** – fontanelle, which is found at the back of the skull, where the **parietal bones** join the **occipital bone**. A more scrupulous study will also reveal the **mastoid** and **sphenoidal** fontanelles.

During birth the fontanelles allow the skull's bones to flex, enabling the infant's head to pass through the narrow birth canal. As the child grows, the skull hardens, and after several months the posterior fontanelle will usually be closed over. The anterior fontanelle takes longer, remaining open until the child is almost two.

The range of medical tests run on a small baby includes the **palpation** of the anterior fontanelle; if it's sunken it may indicate dehydration; while a bulging fontanelle may indicate raised **intracranial pressure**. Fontanelles seem soft and all too easy to damage. But be reassured, the covering membrane is much tougher than it looks.

The Frog

is the builder's term for the hollow in the top of a building brick which holds the mortar.

There are several stories as to why this indentation is called after a small tailless amphibian of the order Anura, but the best and simplest explanation is that the name comes from the **block** or **former** that is placed in the mould when the brick is made – also called a frog. This was originally made of wood, and when wet and covered with clay was supposed to resemble a crouching frog.

Another more colourful tale traces the name back to the ancient Egyptians, who made hollows in the bricks they manufactured of Nile clay, in which they buried live animals as building work progressed. In 1903 millions of skeletons of *Bufo regularis*, the common African frog, were found in the remains of buildings from ancient Egypt on the Giza Plateau.

When building a wall, the frog should always be laid uppermost. This ensures that the **loading** of the wall is evenly spread across its width, rather than being concentrated on to the edges, as happens if the frog is placed facing down.

Bricks are typically laid in **courses** on a **bed** of mortar. The end of each brick is **buttered** with mortar and then pushed against the preceding brick, squeezing the mortar to a width of 10 mm. The brick is then **tapped down** to **level** with the **heel** of the trowel. Excess mortar is scraped off before the next brick is laid. The horizontal joint is called a **bed joint**; the vertical joints are **perpends**.

The ends of the wall are built first, with the level and **verticality** of the bricks continually checked against a taut **string line**, which is moved up as each course is completed.

A Gaff

is a hooked pole traditionally used by fishermen for pulling big fish ashore (or aboard ship).

Once in the fisherman's hands, if the fish is to die it may well be subjected to a blow from the **priest**, the weighted club that is bashed on the fish's head to finish it off.

If, on the other hand, the fish is to live, a **gag** may come in useful, this being the instrument that holds open the fish's jaws while the hook is removed. Subsequently, the fish may be weighed and thrown back, or held in a **seine net**, which hangs upright in the water.

The gaff is now illegal in the UK.

A Gambrel

is a symmetrical, two-sided roof with two slopes
on each side, the upper one shallow, the lower
one steep.

The idea behind the gambrel is to provide the maximum
headspace in the interior of the upper storey, whilst also
having the advantages of a sloped roof. It is not to be
confused with the **gabled** roof, an ordinary two-sided roof
with triangular sections of wall – or gables – at each end.
If a roof has four sides it is called a **hip roof**, and if it has
four sides with a gambrel-like double slope, it is called a
mansard.

　The long strips of metal or other strong, weatherproof
material that cover the joints and angles of a roof are
called **flashing**; this is not to be confused with **flaunching**,
which is the mortar base that holds the chimney pot in
position on top of the chimney stack.

Garage

is a type of **electronic dance music** that developed in the UK in the mid 1990s, initially an up-tempo version of a famous US sound, itself an electronic version of the **soul** and **gospel**-inspired elements of **disco**.

The story begins at the Paradise Garage, a legendary gay club situated in an ex-parking garage in New York City. Opened in 1976, it was presided over until its closure in 1987 by Larry Levan, once described as 'the greatest DJ ever'. Levan was one of those key figures who elevated the disc jockey from the cheesy record-spinner of the 1970s into the god-like figure of later years, acting as producer, remixer and taste-maker – his nights at the Paradise Garage being famously dramatic and memorable. His early death in 1992 only increased the myths built up around him.

Though garage ultimately takes its name from the Paradise Garage, the US version of the sound developed at Zanzibar, a club in Newark, New Jersey, where another influential DJ, Tony Humphries, cultivated what was known at the time as 'the Jersey sound', electronic music that derived from the jazz, soul and gospel traditions.

In the early 1990s, after the peak of **acid house**, a number of UK DJs championed this American sound. In Manchester's Hacienda, Nottingham's Venus, and London's Ministry of Sound, 'house and garage' was the dance music of choice. For a season, the Ministry even persuaded garage godfather Humphries to become a weekly resident.

Gradually the American sound was replaced by a distinctly UK version – with a higher tempo. Not initially given houseroom by the clubs who played US garage, the UK version found a home down the road from the Ministry at Happy Days in the Elephant and Castle, a club that opened at 6 a.m. for hardcore survivors of the previous night. Particularly popular with women, the dress requirement was as little as possible – seriously skimpy outfits above glamour heels. The scene moved to the Arches in Southwark, with a summer outpost at the resort of Ayia Napa in Cyprus. Known initially as 'speed garage' and 'the London sound', as it spread out from the capital it became 'UK garage'.

By 1996, the sound was more mainstream, with records in the charts and the phenomenon starting to be noticed by the media. In 1997 DJs Matt Lamont and Karl Brown – known together as Tuff Jam – took their remixed version of Rosie Gaines's 'Closer Than Close' to no. 4 in the UK charts. By the close of the millennium, garage was the UK's dance music of choice. 'Fill Me In' and 'Sweet Like Chocolate' both reached no. 1.

Electronic dance music describes a set of genres that ultimately derive from 1970s disco music, as well as the more experimental electronic music of bands such as the German Kraftwerk. It is typically put together on a computer using electronic instruments: synthesizers, drum machines and sequencers, and may include **samples**, short extracts from existing pieces of music, often of very different styles. It has a high beat rate, typically 120 to 200 beats per minute, making it particularly appropriate for dancing. With the development of hard-disk recording systems, almost anyone with a home computer could become a musician, leading to the rise of tracks developed by so-called **bedroom bands**.

The sub-genres of dance music are manifold, and include not just garage and house but styles such as **breakbeat, drum and bass, electro, Eurobeat, hip hop, techno** and **trance**, as well as more experimental music such as **glitch, trip-hop** and **IDM (intelligent dance music)**. Having, since the 1990s, taken over most of those clubs that once upon a time rocked to the sound of disco, genres of electronic dance music are sometimes referred to as **club music**.

Musicians Steve Hillage and Miquette Giraudy of the ambient band System 7 have set out a categorization of electronic dance music genres based on beats per minute:

> 60–90 bpm: hip hop and dub
> 90–120 bpm: faster hip hop, big beats, trip-hop
> 120–135 bpm: house
> 135–155 bpm: techno
> 155–180 bpm: drum and bass, jungle
> 180+ bpm: gabber, hardcore

US garage was 120–130 bpm; the UK sound ratcheted it up to 130–140 bpm.

Gari

is the pink pickled ginger that is served on the corner of a sushi tray to accompany sushi.

Its proper purpose is to cleanse the palate between mouthfuls. It also aids digestion. Though it should really be eaten a slice at a time, many Western sushi lovers like to mash it up with the pungent, bright green **wasabi** paste, which is made from green Japanese horseradish, and is there to enhance the flavour of the sushi.

The word sushi is often used in the West for the generic dish of raw fish, but strictly speaking it describes the cooked rice, delicately flavoured with vinegar, which can be topped with vegetables, raw or cooked fish, egg, or even raw meat. The raw fish (or meat) is called **sashimi** and can be served in bite-sized chunks on its own. Thin slices of raw pheasant and duck have historically also been used for sashimi. Crab, shrimp, octopus and eel, by contrast, are generally cooked or marinated before being incorporated into sushi.

There are two main types of sushi, **maki** and **nigiri**. Maki is the familiar sushi roll, where the rice and fish are laid on a sheet of dried seaweed – or **nori** – then rolled up and sliced into a log-like section. Nigiri sushi has one ingredient, such as a slice of raw salmon, sitting on top of an oblong finger of vinegared rice. A form of maki also known as a **handroll** is **temaki**, where the fish and rice come in a cone of nori.

Soy sauce – or **shōyu** – is also often served on the side. This is made from fermented soybeans, wheat and salt, and comes in both light and dark varieties. Dark soy sauce is thicker than light and not as salty. An even darker condiment called **tamari** is wheat-free and more fragrant than soy sauce.

When flavouring nigiri sushi with soy, you should dip only the top, fishy side into the sauce; if you try dipping the rice side you will find it crumbling into an undignified mess.

In Japan, master sushi chefs undergo a prolonged apprenticeship. Starting in his teens, a typical trainee may spend years just watching his master as he selects the freshest fish in the market. Back in the sushi shop, his jobs will include cleaning, washing up and delivering sushi around town; he is unlikely to be let near the actual sushi preparation at this stage. Eventually he will be allowed to watch his master prepare the delicately flavoured rice; then to fan the rice to cool it. Only after ten years or so will he be allowed up to the counter at the front of the shop, as an assistant or **wakiita** (literally, 'side chopping board'). Now he will be allowed to roll sushi and prepare fish for more senior chefs. If he proves himself in this role, he will eventually become an **itamae** (literally, 'in front of the chopping board'), allowed to prepare his own sushi for chosen customers.

A Gasket

is a ring of rubber, asbestos or metal (among other materials) which is shaped to seal the junction between metal surfaces.

In a car engine the **head gasket** is crucial in ensuring a good seal between the **cylinder head** and the **cylinder**. If your car 'blows a gasket' the seal is broken and you are in serious trouble . . .

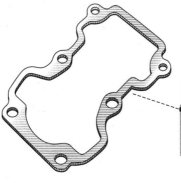

Even though most people drive a car on a regular basis, and could easily distinguish between a Porsche and a Skoda, how many of us have even the faintest idea of the difference between the **cams** and the **crankshaft**, let alone what a **tuned port fuel-injection** might be?

But in actual fact, what lies beneath the **bonnet** of a car is relatively straightforward, and the basic elements of the **internal combustion engine** and its parts can be understood in not much more time than it takes to reverse a car into a tight spot in town.

The internal combustion engine, as its name suggests, is an engine that burns fuel inside itself.* It converts petrol into motion by harnessing the energy from hundreds of tiny explosions per minute, each one of which forces the **piston** down the **cylinder**, rotating the **crankshaft**, which in turn drives the car. Most engines are powered by more than one cylinder, hence terms such as **four-cylinder, eight-cylinder** and so on.

Each explosion begins with a drop of fuel let in through the **intake valve** at the top of the engine. This then mixes with air before being compressed by the upward motion of the piston. The resultant mixture is then ignited by a spark from a **spark plug**, creating an explosion – the combustion – that forces the piston back down. At this point the **exhaust valve** opens, allowing the now contaminated air to escape.

That's basically it – though a lot of other parts are required to make this up-and-down motion run smoothly. **Piston rings** provide a seal between piston and cylinder so that the explosion is contained. The **sump** collects the oil that lubricates the engine and the seal. The separate system that opens and closes the intake and exhaust valves is a **camshaft**. The bit that distributes the electric charge between the four separate spark plugs of a four-cylinder engine is the **distributor**. The **carburettor** mixes the fuel with air before it enters the cylinder.

Many modern engines have swanky varieties of these basic parts, but the essential principle of internal combustion remains the same. Your turbocharged motor may have **double overhead cams, catalytic converters** and a **V-8 cylinder system,** but it's still powered by a series of explosions.

* In contrast to the **external combustion engine,** such as might be seen on a steam train, which burns fuel outside itself.

Glassine

is the type of paper that lines your box of chocolates or truffles, and cups single chocolates as well. It is very thin and light; in a special manufacturing process, paper pulp is beaten to break down the fibres, and pressed into moulds, and then allowed to dry into sheets. Then, in a process called calendering, the sheets are pressed many times through hot rollers, thus delivering a paper that is grease-proof, moisture- and even air-proof, ideal for protecting chocolates from that white 'bloom' that can sometimes appear.

Glassine paper is used to separate slices of foods in vacuum-sealed packets which might normally stick together, such as smoked salmon or Parma ham; it is also used to protect book jackets, and illustrations in antique books.

The uniquely unlovely sound of the kazoo is formed by a vibrating membrane made of glassine paper.

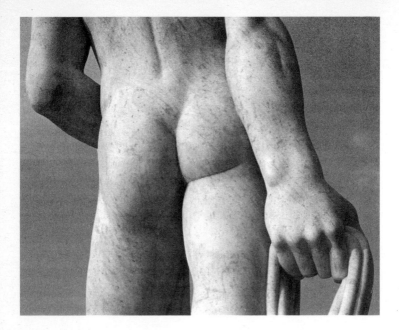

The *Gluteal crease*

is the place where the lower buttocks meet the upper leg.

If those buttocks are particularly comely, they might be described by the adjective **callipygian**, a word which derives from the Greek for beautiful (*kallos*) and buttocks (*pyge*). The Callipygian Venus is a famous marble statue of a female nude, supposedly discovered in the Domus Aurea – a porticoed villa built in Rome by the Emperor Nero – and now displayed at the Museo Nazionale Archeologico in Naples, Italy.

A *Gnomon*

(pronounced Know-mon)

is the triangular-shaped part of a sundial that casts a shadow, the position of which shows the time.

The sundial is the oldest known device for the measurement of time. It is based on the fact that an object's shadow will move from one side of it to the other as the sun moves from east to west during the day. A sundial is believed to have been used in Babylon as early as 2000 BC.

The sun travels 15 degrees of longitude westwards in 1 hour, equivalent to 950 feet per second. So, sunset at Lowestoft, which is the easternmost point of England, is exactly 7 minutes earlier than sunset in Greenwich. Sunset in Penzance, Cornwall, is 22 minutes and 12 seconds later than at Greenwich, and half an hour later than at Lowestoft.

I am a sundial, and I make a botch
Of what is done much better by a watch.

Hilaire Belloc, 'On a Sundial', 1938

A Grawlix

is a sequence of typographical symbols used by cartoonists to represent a swear word. *%!@*$! might be an example.

The cartoonist Mort Walker, creator of *Beetle Bailey*, a long-running US cartoon strip, invented a whole vocabulary to describe the devices cartoonists use in dialogue balloons to represent emotions, obscenities and physical exertions. For example, **agitrons** are wiggly lines indicating that something is shaking. **Briffits** are clouds of dust that hang in the spot where a swiftly departing character or object was previously standing. **Emanata** are

straight lines rising from around a character's head indicating surprise. **Squeans** are asterisks with an empty centre, indicating drunkenness or dizziness. **Plewds** are flying sweat droplets that appear around the head of a character who is working hard or stressed and **waftaroms** are wavy lines rising from something to indicate a strong smell.

In the Tintin books, Captain Archibald (yes, that really is his first name) Haddock's outbursts are always accompanied by grawlix. Some such outbursts are single words – *Artichokes! Hydrocarbon! Cro-magnon!* – and range from the easily understood to the arcane. The old seadog's longer outbursts are generally alliterative. *'Billions of bilious barbecued blue blistering barnacles!'* is a particularly choice example. Sometimes they test the general knowledge not just of a child but an adult too. Haddock's favourite oath of *'Bashi-bazouk!'* refers to the mercenary soldiers employed by the Turkish Ottoman Empire to supplement their fighting forces. *'Pestilential pachyderms!'*, if taken literally, would refer to elephants of a disease-ridden nature, *'Pithecanthropuses!'* would describe fossil hominids and *'Slubberdegullions!'* filthy slobbering people.

A *Grubber*

is a ball bowled **underarm** along the ground in the game of cricket.

Perhaps the easiest of the available options, this method of bowling is often taught to children and beginners. Once a bowler gains experience, however, they will generally not only bowl **overarm**, but use a variety of cunning **pitches** to test the batsman's mettle to the full. Pitching the ball in such a way that it turns from **off*** to **leg** is known as an **off-break**; while if you pitch it the other way round, so it turns from leg to off, that's a **leg-break**.

The much-talked-about **googly** is an off-break cunningly disguised to resemble a leg-break. A **yorker** is a ball that pitches directly at the batsman's feet. A **bouncer** is a fast ball pitched short, so it bounces intimidatingly high. **Body-line**, as the name suggests, is fast bowling directed straight at the batsman.

The batsman, meanwhile, aims to score as many **runs** as possible before losing his **wicket** – whether bowled or being stumped or caught out by one of the ten **fielders** who are situated around him in a variety of descriptive positions, from **silly mid-off** or **square leg** to **long-on** or **deep third man**. One of the words in these positions describes the fielder's angle to the batsman (e.g. **leg, cover, mid-wicket**) another the distance (**silly, short, deep** or **long**). 'Silly' means very close to the batsman.

The batsman may hit the ball far enough away to enable him to make one or more **runs**, or he may score a **bye**, a run taken from a ball that passes the wicket without touching the bat or batsman. If the ball is hit and reaches the boundary line without being stopped by a fielder, it

---

* The half of the field, divided lengthways, towards which the batsman's feet are pointed; leg is the other half.

scores four. If it flies over the boundary line in the air, it scores six. The danger is always of hitting the ball too high and too short, so that you are **caught out**, perhaps in a **dolly** or **sitter**, which are terms for an easy catch.

Sporting relations between Australia and New Zealand reached an all-time low on 1 February 1981 when Australian captain Greg Chappell ordered his brother Trevor to bowl underarm for the final delivery of a limited-overs One Day International at Melbourne Cricket Ground. The Kiwi visitors needed to score a six off this last ball of the match just to tie with the Aussies, hardly an easy prospect at the world's largest cricket ground, and with their no. 10 batsman (Brian McKechnie) at the crease. But the Chappell brothers decided to give him no chance at all by bowling a grubber, a decision that was thought to be mightily unsporting, indeed against the whole spirit of the game. Legendary commentator Richie Benaud described the move as 'disgraceful . . . one of the worst things I have ever seen done on a cricket field'. Subsequently, politicians on both sides of the Tasman Sea became involved in the controversy. New Zealand Prime Minister Rob Muldoon called it 'an act of cowardice . . . I consider it appropriate that the Australian team were wearing yellow,' later adding for good measure that this was 'the most disgusting incident I can recall in the history of cricket'. Even his embarrassed Australian counterpart, Malcolm Fraser, agreed that the incident was 'contrary to the traditions of the game'.

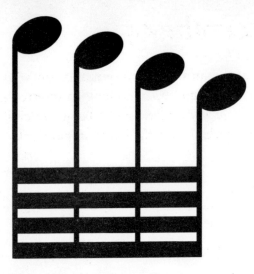

A *Hemidemisemiquaver*

is a note played for one sixty-fourth the duration of a whole note, or **semibreve**.

Half a semibreve is called a **minim,** and half of this, one quarter of a whole note, is a **crotchet,** while one eighth of a whole note is a **quaver**.

Notes shorter than the sixty-fourth note are very rarely used in music, although the **semihemidemisemiquaver**, half the length of a hemidemisemiquaver, is occasionally found. Beethoven used these in the first movement of his piano sonata op.13, the 'Pathétique', composed in 1798.

The *Interrobang*

is one of the most eloquent punctuation marks in the English language, combining an interrogative point, or question mark, and a bang, which is printers' parlance for the exclamation mark.

There are some sentences which require, nay, demand an interrobang:

'She said what?!'
'He ate how many slices of cake?!'
'You're going to have a baby?!'

There have been various attempts to incorporate the two marks into one symbol by graphic designers, but this has never caught on . . .

A *Jabot*

is a ruffle or frill, generally of lace, worn at the throat of a woman's shirt or blouse. Jabots were formerly also worn at the neck of a man's shirt, and still are by Scots wearing traditional Highland Dress.

In the history of fashion, the somewhat ostentatious jabot has generally made an appearance in eras of luxury and ease. It was a key part of the costume of a gentleman in the late eighteenth century, both on this side of the Channel, and at the French court of Louis XVI and Marie Antoinette, where it was worn by both sexes. It made a reappearance in 'La Belle Epoque', the comfortable, pre-war years of Edward VII. In the US at this time, the fashionable 'Gibson girl' would sport a jabot above her ample bosom and tight, neat waist. The frills returned again in the 1960s, as a luxe hippy accessory, and again in the 1980s, where power-dressing women softened their look with a bit of lace at the neck.

Of course in modern times, no one has worn a jabot with quite the panache of a certain Austin Powers . . .

In the world of Interior Decoration, the word jabot also refers to the parts of a curtain that hang down to either side of the central **swag**.

Julienne

is the term which describes one or more vegetables cut into long thin strips and served cooked or raw.

Carrots are commonly julienned before cooking, as are potatoes, though this preparation also goes by the more common name of chips or French fries. Meat and fish can also be julienned, especially for stir-fry dishes.

But 'julienne' is no pretentious modern usage, invented for the extravagantly styled menus of the post *nouvelle cuisine* world, where fish are line-caught, scallops are hand-dived, poultry is organically reared, and everything comes on a bed of rocket or polenta. The first known use of the word is from 1722, in *Le Cuisinier Royal et Bourgeois*, the classic manual for French chefs, which included recipes from the kitchens of 'Sun King' Louis XIV and marked the beginning of *haute cuisine*.

Even the hippest contemporary menus are grounded in old French terms, though the meanings of words have often been radically extended or even changed. A **coulis**, for example, originally referred to the juice of cooked meat; now it is used for all kinds of sauces and purees, from tomato to blackcurrant. An **infusion** literally describes leaves or slices of fruit or vegetable steeped in hot liquid (however fancy the word sounds, we should always remember that a cup of tea is an infusion). **Jus** is simply the French word for juice. And a **roulade** is no more than a roll: a slice of meat, pastry or cake rolled around a filling.

Other smart-sounding French terms have specific and basic meanings: **lyonnaise** means garnished or cooked with onions; **parmentier**, garnished or cooked with potatoes; **provençale**, cooked with garlic and tomatoes; and **Véronique** garnished with white grapes.

Kanji

are the Japanese pictograms, based on Chinese characters, used in the modern Japanese writing system.

There are other sets of Japanese written symbols, representing syllables, called **hiragana** and **katakana**. Kanji are generally used for nouns, adjectives and the stems of verbs; hiragana for the endings of verbs and other grammatical particles; and katakana for non-Japanese words and loan words. When you don't know the kanji, or suspect your reader might not be able to follow a kanji, you may use hiragana instead. The choice of which you use in your writing is dictated by both convention and personal style. The kanji for 'I', or 'me', for example, is: 私. The hiragana for the same thing is: わたし. The kanji 'I' is generally used in formal writing; the hiragana 'I' in informal writing, such as letters or diaries.

When the Japanese language is represented in the Latin alphabet the script is called **rōmaji**. This is used by Western students starting out in the language and also for inputting to computers. So the Japanese for tea, which is お茶 in kanji, is *ocha* in rōmaji.

Traditionally, Japanese was written in a format called **tategaki**, where the characters are placed in columns going from top to bottom, ordered from right to left. As your eyes reach the bottom of a column, you move to the top of the next one on the left. The spine of the book is on the right, so to Western eyes it reads back-to-front. Modern Japanese also uses the **yokogaki** system, where writing is laid out horizontally and reads from left to right.

After the Second World War the Japanese decided to both simplify and restrict their kanji. They ended up with a list of 1,850 approved characters, which has now been expanded to 1,945, considerably fewer than the 3,000 to 4,000 characters needed to get by in Chinese.

It has been said that the Japanese writing system is best understood as the attempt to use Chinese characters to write down a totally different language. *Kan* in fact means 'Chinese' and *ji* means 'character'.

The *Keeper*

is the loop on a belt through which the free end of the belt threads after it has gone through the buckle.

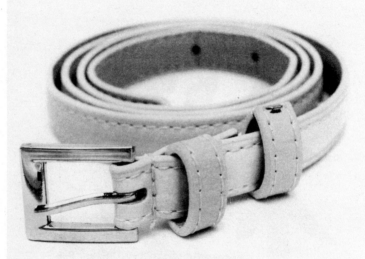

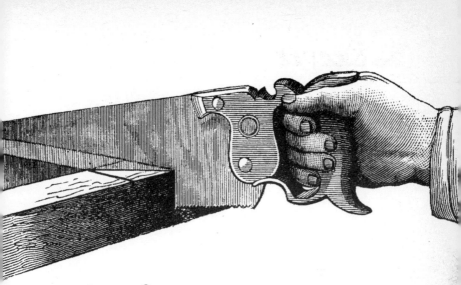

The Kerf

is the groove or notch made by a cutting tool such as a saw.

As the saw cuts the wood, its teeth remove material as sawdust, forming a channel wider than the blade, and making the saw's progress easier through the material being cut.

The size of the saw's teeth determines the smoothness of the cut. The more tooth points per inch of blade, the smoother the cut surface. Most saws used for cutting lumber have 5 to 10 points per inch. For fine work, there are saws with as many as 20 points per inch.

A saw's teeth slant alternately to the left and right. A **crosscut saw** is used to cut across the grain of a board. A **ripsaw** cuts lengthwise with the grain. A **backsaw** will cut both across and with the grain.

The Labret

is the lip piercing your niece just got for her sixteenth birthday.

Or perhaps *you* fancy a horizontal piercing through the bridge of the nose, which is called an **earl**. The helix, which is the name of the outer cartilage ridge of the ear, is a popular location for multiple rings, as is the tragus, the small tab of tissue which projects over the opening of the ear canal.

There's also the **areola nipple ring**, and the **belly button ring** or **stud**. Some people choose very unusual sites for their piercings, like the uvula at the back of the throat opening, or they might go for a **scrumper**, which is a piercing of the thin webbing between the upper teeth and lip.

Your choice . . .

None of these piercings is quite so intrusive, nor, one would imagine, so painful, as the **lip plate**, which is a required

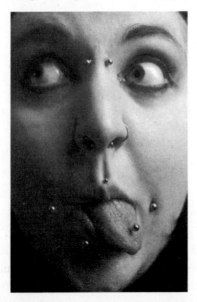

adornment in certain African tribes. Only women have this accessory; the bigger the plate, the wealthier the man they can attract.

A *Lavaliere*

(pronounced Lav-uh-leer)

is the jeweller's term for a pendant on a fine chain that is worn as a necklace.

It is named after the Duchesse de la Vallière, the first of the many mistresses of Louis XIV. She was his 'official mistress' between 1661 and 1667 and bore him six children.

In a modern adaptation of this word, a lavalier microphone is the name for the type of mic that slips on to the shirt or tie of an interview subject. The advantage of such a device is that it filters out some of the ambient noise in the studio that a stationary mic would include.

A *Loupe*

is a magnifying glass used in professions where
a method of close inspection is needed.

For those whose work requires them to have both hands
free, loupes are often worn as an attachment to spectacles.
You may have seen surgeons, dentists or photographers
using them.

Jewellers employ a loupe that magnifies ten times to
examine flaws and cuts in diamonds. If no defects can
be seen at that level of magnification, the diamond is
considered to be in good condition. (The key thing to
remember when selecting diamonds are the four Cs:
cut, colour, clarity and carat.)

Perhaps the most glamorous appearance of a loupe is in
those TV shots of engravers waiting for the results at
Wimbledon, Wembley or Wentworth, while the final
moments of the tournament are being played out – and the
name to be engraved on the trophy still hangs in the
balance.

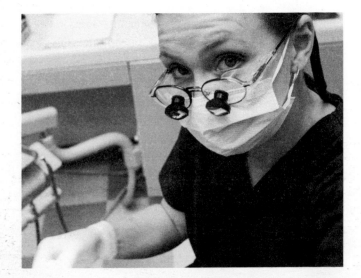

A *Louvre*

(pronounced Loo-ver)

is the angled slat that is hung or fixed at regular intervals to make up a shutter, blind or screen.

Designed to admit light and air, but exclude rain, they are often to be seen on the upper windows of church towers, where collectively they make up the **bell screen,** covering the bells in the **belfry.**

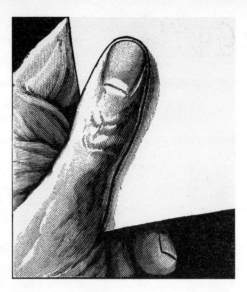

The *Lunula*

is the white half-moon part of the nail plate at the base of the toe- and fingernails. It is a paler colour than the rest of the nail because it isn't so firmly attached to the blood vessels.

This feature tends to be most visible on the thumbs, but not everyone has visible lunulae, so don't panic if you can't see yours right now.

The thick fold of skin that overlaps the lunula, which the manicurist pushes down, is called the **eponychium**, the anatomical name for the **cuticle**; its function is to protect the area between the nail and the skin from exposure to harmful bacteria.

The nails can give warning signs of certain diseases and disorders: for example, brittle nails could indicate iron deficiency, thyroid problems or impaired kidney function, and pitting of the nails is associated with psoriasis.

The MacGuffin

is the object, event or character in a film or story that serves to set and keep the plot in motion.

Alfred Hitchcock came up with the name in a 1939 lecture he gave at Columbia University. 'In crook stories,' he said, 'it is most always the necklace, and in spy stories it is most always the papers.' The 'government secrets' in *North by Northwest* and the 'secrets vital to your air defence' in *The 39 Steps* are both Hitchcockian MacGuffins, and MacGuffins can be detected in other films too: the jewel-encrusted sculpture of a falcon in *The Maltese Falcon*, or the briefcase – the contents of which we never discover, nor need know – in *Pulp Fiction*.

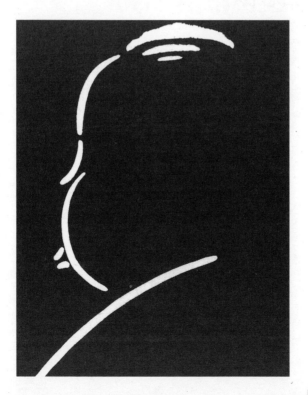

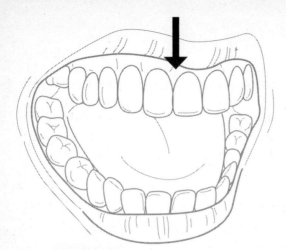

The Maxillary central incisor

is one of the most prominent teeth in the mouth, which sits with its matching twin bang in the middle of the front upper jaw or **maxilla**. As with all incisors its function is to cut your food as you chew it.

Flanking these two on either side are the **maxillary lateral incisors**. Next, from front to back, are the **canines** (used for tearing), the first and second **premolars** and the first, second and third **molars**, which are flat teeth, used for chewing. The third molar is also commonly called the wisdom tooth, and may remain below the gum or only erupt late in life. The teeth on the lower jaw, or **mandible**, have the same names, but with the prefix **mandibular**.

On a visit to the dentist, you are highly unlikely to hear the full names of these teeth being called out to the nurse as your check proceeds. Instead, your dentist will follow one of three systems of notation. The Palmer system, still generally used in the UK, divides the teeth into four quadrants – upper right, upper left, lower left and lower right – with teeth numbered 1 to 8 within each. Your check will start with upper right and end at lower right. The incisors are numbers 1 and 2 in all quadrants.

In the FDI World Dental Federation notation (ISO-3950 notation), which is supposed to have superseded the Palmer system, the first number designates the quadrant and the second the tooth within it. So the upper right incisors are 12 and 11 and the lower right 41 and 42. This system is more likely to be used by the dentist in written communication, when instructing technicians or making referrals to other dentists.

In the Universal system, commonly used in the USA, adult teeth are numbered from 1 to 32.

The famous song 'All I Want For Christmas Is My Two Front Teeth' was written by the American lyricist Don Yetter Gardner in 1944, while teaching music at an elementary school in Smithtown, New York. Having asked the children in his Grade 2 class what they wanted for Christmas, Gardner noticed that many lisped their answers, their deciduous maxillary central incisors not having yet been replaced by their permanent ones.

Wisely avoiding the use of the correct terminology, Gardner's song achieved huge popularity, recorded down the years by artists from Nat King Cole to Mariah Carey. The 1984 Spike Jones version reached no. 1 and sold nearly a million and a half copies in seven weeks.

Gardner died on 15 September 2004, at the age of ninety-one. He was still receiving royalties from the fun little song he'd penned over half a century earlier.

Metonymy

is one of the best-known **figures of speech** and one many of us use most days, especially if we read or quote from the tabloids. It means, simply, substituting an attribute of the thing you're talking about for the thing itself. A good example is saying 'the Crown', when we mean the Queen; or 'the Turf', when we mean horse racing. Or we might talk about a 'tongue' to mean a language; or a 'dish', when we mean the food served up on that dish.

Figures of speech are traditionally divided into two kinds: **schemes** and **tropes**. Schemes (from the Greek *schema*, a form or shape) involve changing the pattern of words from what you would ordinarily expect. 'Full many a glorious morning I have seen' is a scheme, because it switches round, in a poetic way, the altogether more pedestrian: 'I have seen a great many glorious mornings'. And with good reason: because who would hang around to listen to the rest of a speech that began like that? That particular scheme is a **rhetorical inversion** called **anastrophe**.

Tropes, on the other hand, involve changing the *general meaning* of a word or term. The classic example of a trope is **irony**, whereby a word is used to convey the opposite of its usual meaning. 'Beautiful day, isn't it?' we say as it pours with rain, but of course it's not beautiful at all, we're using the word ironically, to mean something very different. **Litotes** is another form of trope, whereby an idea is conveyed by negating its opposite. 'He's not exactly sober,' we say of a friend, and thereby get across, in an understated way, that he's horribly drunk. Once again, the meaning of the key word 'sober' has changed.

Some other figures of speech:
- **Antonomasia** – the use of a name to convey a general idea about a person. 'He's a terrible old Scrooge,' we say, referring to the famous old miser in Charles Dickens's *A Christmas Carol*. Or: 'You're a right little Einstein, aren't you?' meaning that you're rather too good at maths to be bearable.
- **Euphemism** – the use of a mild, vague or inoffensive expression instead of a harsher or more explicit one. 'She passed away,' we say. 'She popped her clogs.' 'She's pushing up the daisies.' Or, on another tricky subject: 'I got to first base', 'I did the wild thing',

'We indulged in some carnal gymnastics.' All are ways of rephrasing the blunt basics of 'She died,' or 'I had sex.'

◆ **Hyperbole** – exaggeration or overstatement in order to emphasize. 'I could eat a horse,' you say, as you sit down in front of a ploughman's lunch or a baked potato. The idea that you might eat, even if it were offered, a few slices of horse carpaccio, let alone a whole horse, is ridiculous, but the metaphor works.

◆ **Oxymoron** – the linking of incongruous or contradictory terms for effect. 'The most intelligent idiot in Parliament,' we might say of a particularly effective MP. And from this simple linkage come all sorts of wonderful extra meanings. That everyone in Parliament is of course an idiot. That this person in particular stands out. That raw intelligence itself does not necessarily mean that someone is wise, canny, streetwise or in other ways worth listening to.

◆ **Synecdoche** – a form of metonymy: the substitution of the part for the whole. We talk about 'new faces' at a meeting, when obviously the faces would never get to the meeting in the first place if they weren't somehow joined to the floor and given life support by all the other parts of the body. 'All hands on deck' would be another example of synecdoche.

◆ **Zeugma** – using one adjective or verb with two nouns, one of which it applies to directly, the other figuratively. 'We watched Diana's coffin pass with tearful eyes and hearts,' wrote one tabloid journalist of the Princess's funeral. Obviously you can't literally have a tearful heart, but the metaphorical point is clear.

The *Mirror band*

is the ring just inside the main printable area of a compact disc.

It is etched with the name of the manufacturer, as well as a number of barcode identifications. Because the mirror band is not encoded with other data, it has a different reflective quality, appearing both shinier and darker than other parts of the disc. It is not to be confused with the **stacking ring,** on the underside, which is the very thin circle of raised plastic that prevents the surface of the CD being scratched when discs are piled up.

A *compact disc is made* from polycarbonate plastic; a thin layer of aluminium is applied to one surface to make it reflective, which is then protected by a film of lacquer. Information is stored on the CD as a series of tiny indentations called **pits** and **lands,** which are contained in a tightly packed **spiral track.** To retrieve the information a laser beam is focused on the track and the CD player's detector – or **photodiode** – senses the difference between the light reflected from each, before turning this into an electrical signal. CDs hold huge amounts of information; one second of audio requires a million bits of data.

The first commercially released CD was Abba's *The Visitors*, in August 1982. Ironically, as the CD was being launched Abba were splitting up – this was to be their last album. It's certainly a melancholy listen: both sets of partners were divorcing each other, and the songs have lyrics about failed relationships, ageing, and the loss of innocence.

Dire Straits was the first group to sell a million copies in CD format, with their 1985 album *Brothers In Arms*. The rise of the CD tolled the death knell for 8-track tapes, and, eventually, for vinyl. Now the future of the CD itself is unclear, as increasing numbers of music-lovers download their choice of artists straight from the internet.

A *Moonbow*

is the nocturnal equivalent of a rainbow.

Just as there are rainbows during the day, there can be moonbows at night. Both rainbows and moonbows are created by light being scattered inside small water droplets, typically from nearby rainfall – although mist, spray, dew, fog, and ice can also be conduits. Each droplet acts as a miniature prism; many together create the picturesque spectrum of colours that is the rainbow.

Because the moon gives out relatively little light compared to the sun, moonbows aren't as bright as rainbows. The colour-receptors in our eyes aren't sufficiently excited to see all the prismatic colours, so generally the moonbow appears to be white.

Your best chance to see a moonbow is to stand with the moon at your back. If there is the right kind of moisture in the air, you will see the ghostly bow ahead of you.

So we'll go no more a-roving
So late into the night,
Though the heart still be as loving,
And the moon still be as bright.

For the sword outwears its sheath,
And the soul outwears the breast,
And the heart must pause to breathe,
And love itself have rest.

Though the night was made for
    loving,
And the day returns too soon,
Yet we'll go no more a-roving
By the light of the moon.

(George Gordon) Lord Byron, 1817

The *Muffin top*

is an increasingly common sight on the high street, as people's average weight continues to increase.

The recipe for this look is very simple. Wear one tight-fitting pair of low-rise hip-hugging jeans, add a crop top that exposes a large expanse of midriff, and mix with an excess of poundage.

Voilà! The surplus flesh and fat will flop over the waistline of the jeans, rather in the way a muffin top spills over its paper casing.

And – let's not be sexist about this – men can easily achieve the same look too . . .

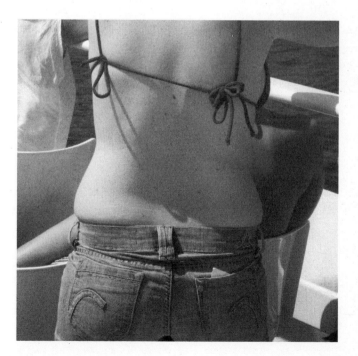

A *Mule*

is a sterile crossbreed between a horse and a donkey. But in the world of women's fashion, it's the name for a backless shoe (or slipper), sometimes without a heel.

These accessories are much worn by modern heroines of chick-lit, who always seem to be slipping out of bed and into a pair of mules. In the US, where they were favourites of the leading characters of *Sex and the City*, these shoes are known as **slides**.

The word as it applies to shoes * comes from the ancient Sumerian *mulu*, meaning an indoor shoe without a back or heel. Adopted first by the Egyptians, who added a heel so they could be worn outdoors, mules arrived in France in the seventeenth century, where they were known as *mulettes*, and regarded as chic and provocative.

Slippers returned as a fashion item in the teens and twenties of the twentieth century. Risqué new dances such as the tango and the Maxixe were performed at *thés dansants* in daring new slippers: beaded, jewelled, ribboned and buckled.

Mules made something of a comeback in the fifties, with Marilyn Monroe wearing a pair in *The Seven Year Itch*. They subsequently languished during the sixties and seventies, before returning triumphantly in the 1990s in the designs of Manolo Blahnik, Donna Karan, Emma Hope and Patrick Cox. The Czech-Spanish designer Blahnik in particular was associated with unconventional and exotic mules – known to some of his fans1 as 'Manolos'.

---

* It has no relation to the word for the animal, which comes from a Latin root.

142 MULE

Though often approving of the effect that particular footwear has on the appearance of their womenfolk, many men go through life without a full grasp of the names of these shoes. The average guy may admire the lift a stiletto gives to his girlfriend's backside, but would he be able to define accurately the difference between a **kitten heel** and a **court shoe**?

Here are some of the key shoe varieties:

- **Clog** – a thick-soled shoe made from hardwood. The original Dutch clog is simply a block of wood which has been hollowed out and shaped to fit the foot. The English clog has a wooden sole with an upper made of leather, canvas or even raffia.

- **Court shoes** – heeled shoes with low-cut fronts and usually no fastening. They are typically black, and said to take their style and name from the footwear worn at the twelfth-century court of Queen Eleanor of

Aquitaine. Similar shoes were also worn with stockings and knee-breeches by men at court in the nineteenth century (and still are by judges today). In the 1920s, designers started adding decoration to the court shoe: ornamental buckles and even glass balls followed.

◆ A **kitten heel** is a heel of 5 cm or less in height. Classified as 'high heels', kittens took off in the 1950s as trainer shoes for adolescent girls. Later, they became sexy adult wear in their own right.

◆ **Platform shoes** raise the ball of the foot as well as the heel. The soles are made from cork or manmade styrene and range from half an inch to eight inches in thickness. Heel and sole are generally two separate units. Platforms were invented in the 1930s by the French designer Roger Vivier, and became an American craze in the 1940s. Out of fashion for twenty years after the war, platforms staged a comeback in 1968, when the 'trendy' store Biba launched a suede boot with a five-inch heel.

◆ **Pumps** are flat or low-heeled shoes of the kind dancers wear. You might even call plimsolls or gym shoes pumps. Beware when travelling to the US, however. Over there they use the word pumps for court shoes.

◆ A **slingback** is a court shoe with an adjustable strap at the back, rather than a straightforward quarter.

◆ With its tall, thin, spiked heel, the **stiletto** is a relative newcomer to the world of shoes. Though high heels have been worn for centuries, the stiletto didn't appear till the mid 1950s, when advances in technology allowed a thin, metal, weight-supporting shaft to be inserted within such a narrow heel. A woman in stilettos is said to exert greater pressure on the floor or ground through her heels than would an elephant standing on one foot.

◆ Like the platform shoe, the **wedge** uses a chunky cork or styrene sole to raise the foot, but it's generally linked in one piece with the heel. Wedges were patented in Italy in 1936 by Salvatore Ferragamo, after the steel he usually used for soles had become unobtainable during the war with Abyssinia (1935–6). By the end of that decade these substitute shoes were all the rage.

Platforms, high heels and stilettos can all trace their origins back to the **chopines** worn by aristocratic ladies in sixteenth-century Venice, backless, slipper-type shoes mounted on cylinders that could be as high as a balance-defying thirty inches – though women wearing such grotesque footwear were generally supported by a maid on either side. In 1430, a law had been passed in Venice banning the chopine, but they continued to be worn. In Shakespeare's *Hamlet*, the eponymous hero tells Gertrude, 'Your ladyship is nearer to heaven than when I saw you last, by the altitude of a chopine.'

'Any woman who, through the use of high-heeled shoes or other devices, leads a subject of Her Majesty into marriage, shall be punished with the penalties of witchery.'

Act of Parliament, 1600s

The *Muselets*

is the four-legged wire cage that is wound around the neck and over the cork of a champagne bottle.

At the top of the muselets is an embossed tin **capsule**, which some people collect, either as a reminder of the make and vintage of the champagne itself or simply as a memento of a wonderful evening.

To match the bubbles with the celebration, it's always useful to know the different champagne-bottle sizes:

Piccolo	quarter bottle
Demi-boîte	half bottle
Standard	750ml full bottle
Magnum	2 bottles
Jeroboam	4 bottles
Rehoboam	6 bottles
Methuselah	8 bottles
Salmanazar	12 bottles
Balthazar	16 bottles
Nebuchadnezzar	20 bottles
Melchior	24 bottles
Sovereign	33.33 bottles

If, on the other hand, your tipple is beer, you should perhaps know that a barrel is defined as a container able to hold 36 gallons of ale.

A *Niqaab*

(pronounced nick-cab)

is a head-covering worn by Muslim women which conceals the face entirely, leaving only a narrow slit for the eyes.

A less comprehensive version, the **half-niqaab**, is tied on at the bridge of the nose and covers the lower face. Another addition is the **betula**, the beak-like covering for the nose, generally made of cloth with a metallic sheen. The **bushiyya**, by contrast, is a veil that has no cut-out slit for the eyes; instead the fabric is sheer enough to be seen through.

In western Europe, the niqaab has recently attracted much controversy. In the UK it was famously objected to by Jack Straw, MP for Blackburn, who went on record as saying that to cover facial features in this way was 'bound to make better, positive relations between the two communities more difficult'. He was referring to the white indigenous and Pakistani groups in his Yorkshire constituency.

There are other head coverings and veils worn by Muslim women that are less obscuring. The South Asian **dupatta** (also known as the **shayla** or **milfeh**) is worn with the loose **salwar kameez** trouser suit; wrapped around the head, it leaves the face open. The **hijab** has a similar effect, but is made up of a square of fabric folded into a triangle which is secured under the chin. (The word hijab can be used equally to describe the headscarf, the entire dress of the Muslim woman, or a curtain; and by extension any separation between men and women.)

Below the neck, the rest of the body is also often covered up by a loose outer garment generally known as a **chador** or **abaya**. In Iran, chadors were traditionally white or light-coloured, and black was avoided because of connotations with death. Since the Islamic Revolution of Ayatollah Khomeini, however, black is regarded as the proper colour for a chador.

Elsewhere in the Middle East, black was the traditional colour for the abaya in many Arab countries. In Afghanistan, a heavier version is called the **chadri** – more widely known as the **burqa**; the Taliban during their period of rule between 1996 and 2001 required women to wear burqas in public. The chadri generally comes in blue, with a cloth grille over the face for the woman to look through.

The veiling of women was widespread in the eastern
Mediterranean long before the rise of Islam, a practice
adopted by both Jews and Christians. It wasn't until the
fifth year of the Hijra (626–7 CE) that Muhammad
received a revelation about wrapping up women 'so that
they be recognized and not molested'. After the Prophet's
death, veiling was adopted by middle- and upper-class
Muslim women and by the Middle Ages the niqaab was an
essential part of the feminine wardrobe.

Whether women should wear the veil, or adopt the
unveiled state known as **sufur**, has been an issue in the
Muslim world for well over a century. In 1899, the male
intellectual Qasim Amin published a famous book calling
for freedom for women, *Tahrir al-Mar'a* (The Liberation of
the Woman). In this, Amin advocated sufur as a necessary
step towards social progress for women. He was roundly
criticized by other writers, but women were already
emancipating themselves, with upper-class Egyptians
following the example of Turkish women by wearing
transparent veils, and pioneering feminists such as
Nabawiyya Musa unveiling completely.

In 1923 something of a turning point was reached
when the celebrated Egyptian feminist Huda Sha'rawi
threw her veil into the sea after attending a women's
conference in Rome. As she arrived by train in Cairo, she
repeated the symbolic gesture, drawing back her face veil
to the cheers of her supporters. Others followed, and soon
the veil had all but disappeared from educated Egyptian
society, retained only by women lower down the social
scale (though peasant women had never worn it). In other
Arab countries, such as Morocco and Saudi Arabia,
however, the veil continued to be worn.

But the idea of female modesty in public places wasn't

yet finished with. In the late twentieth century, *al-zayy al-Islami* (Islamic attire) made a dramatic comeback. In part this was due to the rise of Islamist movements advocating a return to traditional Islamic values. But other influences played a part. In one recent Egyptian survey, 40 per cent of women who wore hijab said that they did so because it was fashionable; and in the US they even talk of 'hijab chic'. Others adopted Islamic dress as a form of rebellion, either against liberal, pro-West parents, or as a form of political protest against secular governments.

'The Prophet himself said that the best veil is the veil behind the eyes. Let her be judged by her character and her mind, not by her clothing.'

Sir Shahnawaz Bhutto on appropriate dress for his daughter Benazir

NIQAAB

The *Noctilucent*

is a particularly unusual and magnificent kind of cloud. It can be seen only in the evening, high in the upper reaches of the atmosphere. Whereas normal clouds are found in the **troposphere**, which is the bottom eight miles of the atmosphere, noctilucent clouds are located in the **mesosphere**, which extends up to fifty miles from ground level. Being so high, they can still catch the sun's rays some considerable time after the sun has sunk below the horizon for an observer at ground level, so you can see them glowing a kind of ghostly, blue-white colour in the night sky, usually in wave-like, billowy formations.

Traditionally they are a phenomenon of polar regions, but they're beginning to appear more frequently in other areas of the world too, and you can now see them across the whole of Britain in the months just before and after midsummer.

The *Oche*

(pronounced *okee*)

is the line you must stand behind to throw your arrows in a game of darts.

It's generally located 2.37 metres from the **face** of the dartboard and is also known as the **throw line**. The playable area of the board is called the **island**. Miss it and you are 'off the island'.

This is by no means the only slang relating to the game of darts. The **spider** is the metal web that covers the main board, dividing it into sections. The board itself is often known as the **clock**, as in 'round the clock'. The **cork** is the centre of the board; this dates back to the days when the ends of kegs of beer were used for dartboards, so the cork would be found in the middle.

As for the arrows themselves, the **flight** is the correct name for the back end of a dart, which has the function of stabilizing the dart's trajectory as it flies. The flight is attached to the main **barrel** by the slimmer **shaft** and is also known as the **feathers**. There are many varieties of flight, each with a different shape. Pictured is the **standard**, but you may also find the **heart**, the **kite**, the **pear**, the **axis**, the **combat**, the **fantail** and the **V-wing**.

Scoring in a game of darts is done in reverse, starting from a set 301 or 501 and ending up with exactly zero, a process which is known as **doubling out**. Over the years darts players have evolved a rich private language to describe the different manoeuvres and scores in the average game.

The numbers that have earned themselves a slang nickname are 1, known as **Annie's room** or the **nail**; the double 3, which is the **basement**; the treble 6, called all too obviously the **devil**, and the 20, known as the **double top**.

Common scores also come in for names. A **breakfast** or **chips** is a score of 26, made up of a 20, a 5 and a 1, often got accidentally by players aiming for the 20 and landing either side; when you hit the trebles of these three it's a **champagne breakfast**. A **bag of nuts** is a score of 45, a **baby ton** is 95, and a **high ton** a score higher than 150. Three triple 20s, a score of 180, is called, logically enough, the **maximum**.

A **scroat** is a dart that's aimed for treble 20, but ends up in double 20; a **shanghai** is a score of a single, double and triple in the same number. **Right house, wrong bed** is when you hit a double or triple, but not in the number you wanted. If you lose a game without ever scoring in it you're **skunked**.

Payot

are the long sidelocks worn by Orthodox Jewish men.

Sometimes they are curled, and worn hanging in front of the ear, but generally they are tucked behind the ear or under a broad-brimmed hat or a **yarmulke** (skullcap).

These deeply religious people are obeying the commandment in Leviticus that states: 'Ye shall not round the corners of your heads, neither shalt thou mar the corners of thy beard.'

The *Philtrum*

is the vertical indentation between the upper lip and nose.

The word derives from the Greek *philein*, to kiss or embrace; for the ancient Greeks believed that the philtrum was one of the most erogenous spots on the human body.

It's a curious part of the face, because although a very prominent feature, it seems to serve no useful purpose. One lovely story derives from a passage in the Talmud, the collection of ancient writings that makes up the basis of Jewish religious law. God sends an angel to each womb who teaches a baby all the wisdom it will ever need to know. Shortly before the baby is born, the angel returns, and puts a celestial finger to the baby's face, just between the nose and the upper lip, after which it forgets everything. The philtrum is the indent left by the angel's finger.

Is it attractive? Is it useful? It's certainly true that some of our most striking celebrities (such as Cary Grant and Jennifer Lopez) have pronounced philtrums; also that both dictators and comedians – step forward Charlie Chaplin, Oliver Hardy, Adolf Hitler and Robert Mugabe – have chosen to grow their moustaches just to philtrum width.

Phloem bundles

(pronounced flo-em bundles)

are the squidgy, stringy bits which run between the skin and the edible portion of a banana.

The banana is the fourth most consumed fruit in the world, after grapes, citrus fruits and the apple. Bananas contain three natural sugars – sucrose, fructose and glucose – which give an instant energy boost.

It may look as if bananas grow on trees, because the central stem is upright and sturdy, but in fact this stalk is a **pseudostem** and the 'banana tree' is a herbaceous plant.

As well as providing food, the banana plant has long been a source of fibre for textiles. In Japan, the cultivation of banana for clothing dates back at least to the thirteenth century. The outermost, coarsest fibres of the shoots were used to make rough cloth, while the softest inner fibres were kept for the weaving of kimonos.

A *Phosphene*

is a sensation of light caused by excitation of the
retina rather than by light itself.

Phosphenes are generally caused by touching or rubbing
closed eyes. 'Seeing stars' is a common way of describing
another variety of this phenomenon, which may come after
a blow to the head, a vigorous sneeze, or even low blood
pressure. An upcoming migraine headache is guaranteed to
produce a fine display of phosphenes.

A *Pickguard*

is a protective piece of material under the strings of a guitar, which protects the finish of the guitar's surface from being damaged by the **pick** or **plectrum**. It can be made of plastic, tortoiseshell, mother-of-pearl, ivory, amber, abalone or diamond. After all – this is rock 'n' roll.

Classical guitars don't generally have a pickguard, as they are finger-picked, so not likely to be scratched so much. The Flamenco guitar, however, is often strummed heavily, as well as being tapped with long-nailed fingers, so it has a protective rosette all round the sound-hole, called a **golpeador**.

Pips

are the little dots, or spots – as they're commonly
but incorrectly called – on gambling dice.
Dominoes also have pips, and the diamonds,
hearts, spades and clubs on the ace to the ten
of each suit in a pack of playing cards are called
pips too.

On most dice, the pips consist of small indentations, which
can make for a tiny bias, as more of the die is drilled out
of the faces with higher numbers. So dice used in casinos
have their pips filled with a paint which has the same
density as the acetate the dice are made from – to maintain
a perfect balance.

Dice have always been tampered with – in the time-dishonoured tradition of 'loaded dice'. There are numerous ingenious methods to ensure they land with a selected side facing upwards. If the dice are not transparent, weights can be added to one side, or a drop of mercury put into two linked reservoirs within the die, so it always falls on the same face. Some loaded dice have magnets inserted into them, which are then attracted to a wire hidden in the gaming table.

Modern dice are almost all made of transparent acetate, which makes hiding such dodgy devices within the die much more difficult; and casino dice are each stamped with a serial number to prevent a cheat from substituting a die.

The likelihood of different numbers being obtained by the throw of two dice offers a good introduction to the concept of probability. For the throw of a single die, all outcomes are equally probable. But in the throw of two dice, the total sums are not equally probable. For example, there are six ways to get a 7, but only one way to get a 2, so the odds of getting a 7 are six times those for getting 'snake eyes'. Throwing a 3 is twice as likely as throwing a 2 because there are two ways to get a 3.

The *Pistil*

is the bulbous-headed stalk that you can see at the very centre of a flower. It contains one or more **carpels,** the female part of the plant, made up of **stigma, style** and **ovary.**

The stigma is the head or tip of the pistil, and is generally sticky in order to hold on to the pollen brought on the wind, or by insects and other visiting creatures. The style is the stalk that supports it, down which pollen tubes extend to reach the ovary, which contains the **ovules.** Pollen and ovules combine to produce the **seed.**

Surrounding the pistil are usually the male parts of the flower, the **stamens,** which consist of a **filament** on which is mounted the pollen-producing **anther** (the bit that you should keep well away from white clothes if you want to avoid a stain). Around these are the petals, whose bright colours and scent help to attract insects, who are often also after the nectar to be found in glands called **nectaries.** Outside these are the green **sepals,** which protect the flower before it blooms.

As a group, the whorl of sepals is called the **calyx;** and that of the petals the **corolla.** The male parts of the flower

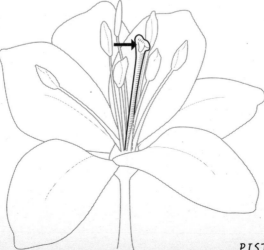

are the **androecium** (from the Greek for 'man's house'); the female parts the **gynoecium** (from the Greek for 'woman's house'). Most flowers contain both male and female parts; they are, in essence, bisexual, and botanists describe them as being **hermaphrodite** or **perfect**. Those flowers which contain only male or only female parts are called **imperfect**.

Carl Linnaeus, the eighteenth-century Swedish natural historian who first classified plants by – amongst other things – counting their pistils and stamens, shocked many of the scientists of his day by his colourful descriptions of the reproductive life of plants. In one piece of writing, he referred to the calyx as 'the bedroom'. In the flower head of a lily, he wrote, 'one wife frolicked with six husbands', while tulip trees enjoyed 'twenty males or more in the same marriage'. Marigolds were promiscuous; their flowers contained 'husbands that live with wives and concubines'.

Despite all the criticism that this provocative rudery provoked, Linnaeus's classification of both animals and plants remains the basis of how we understand and name the natural world today. Absurdly long scientific names for plants were reduced to simple **binomials**, where the name of the genus was followed by that of the species. The common tomato, for example, previously called *Solanum caule inermi herbaceo, foliis pinnatis incisis, racernis simplicibus*, was reduced to the altogether more manageable *Solanum lycopersicum*. Even now Linnaeus's book *Species plantarum* (1753) is the agreed international bible of plant names; and a capital L after a plant name signifies that Linnaeus first assigned it.

The *Plough*

is the British name for a group of seven stars that are prominent in the night sky throughout the winter in the northern hemisphere.

In the US it's known as the Big Dipper, a culinary idea of its appearance that's also picked up in France, where it's called the Casserole. The Germans, by contrast, see it much as we do, calling it the Great Cart. In Finland it's known as Otava and is much used as a cultural symbol. In the Hindu astronomy of India it's Sapta Rishi, meaning the Seven Sages.

The Plough is technically an **asterism**, or smaller star group within a larger constellation; in this case that of Ursa Major (or Great Bear).

Ursa Major is one of 88 official **constellations**, some of which are better known than others. Most sky-watchers can point out Orion the Hunter, with his bright belt of three stars and his attached hunting dog Sirius. Also, perhaps, Aries, the Ram; Cancer, the Crab; Gemini, the Twins; Scorpius, the Scorpion; and Ursa Minor, the Little Bear.

Twelve constellations lie in that part of the sky – the **ecliptic** – through which the sun moves during the year. These are the **zodiac constellations**, so important to astrologers. The original Babylonian zodiac consisted of eighteen signs; but subsequently twelve were assigned a particular month each and in the second century BC the Greek astronomer/astrologer Ptolemy named them all after animals and mythical creatures. These are the ones we know today, though under their Latin names. Zodiac, incidentally, is Greek for 'circle of the animals'.

The boundaries of the constellations weren't set until as late as 1930, when an agreement on the final 88 was reached by the International Astronomical Union. At this time the IAU also recognized a thirteenth zodiacal constellation, Ophiuchus (the serpent-bearer), which sits in the ecliptic between Scorpius and Sagittarius, but is not counted as a sign by astrologers as it doesn't fit into the neat system of twelve signs dividing the ecliptic into twelve equal sections of 30 degrees each.

The stars in most constellations have absolutely no relationship to each other astrophysically, often lying many light years apart in space. The bright stars which make up the Plough, however, are an interesting exception to this rule, since five of them are relatively close in distance, and form what is known as the Ursa Major Moving Group. These are Merak, Phecda, Megrez, Alioth and Mizar, respectively 79, 84, 81, 81 and 78 light years from Earth. The stars at either end of the group, Dubhe and Alkaid, are considerably further away, 124 and 101 light years respectively. They are moving in the opposite direction from the main Ursa Major group and in due course (50,000 years) the Plough will cease to exist, resembling, if anything, a rather bent-handled ladle facing the other way.

The *Poof point*

is the highest point of a pillow or soft cushion when each corner – known as the **nib** – lies flat on a surface. The poof point is inevitably at its best after it has been shaken, patted, prodded and generally jzujzed up.

The type of pillow on which you choose to lay your weary head is, of course, a very important decision, and the type of filling is crucial. Cotton? Foam? Feathers? Or how about down, the fine layer of soft fluff under the main feathers? Buckwheat and millet hulls are very popular these days in the United States.

Whichever you choose, it's always worth remembering that ancient and venerable Hindu saying: 'The softest pillow is a clean conscience . . .'

A *Purlicue*

is a measure of distance marked by the extension of the forefinger and the thumb.

What could be more convenient than using various parts of your body to measure things? The human foot was the origin of the unit called a 'foot', at a time when sophisticated measuring devices did not exist. However, if you take out a ruler, 12 inches is a pretty long foot. Lengths became a lot more accurate when standardization of measurements began more than seven centuries ago.

A **hand** was originally based on the breadth of a man's hand, but is now standardized at 4 inches. It's mainly used to measure the height of horses, taken from the ground to the top of the withers. So a 17-hand horse would be 68 inches high. Fractions of the hand are counted in inches, so a horse of 70 inches would be 'seventeen two'.

The *Quoin*

is the stone that sits at the top – or apex – of an arch. It is often larger than the other stones, and may be decorated in some way; it is also known as the **headstone** or **keystone**.

The other slightly tapered stones around the arch are called **wedgestones** or **voussoirs**. The lowermost voussoir on each side is the **springer**. Below that, supporting the arch on each side, is the **pier**. The word voussoir comes from the French for a 'turn', as each stone turns the thrust of the mass above until the horizontal line of the springer transfers the weight to the pier. The sections to left and right of the arch, between the curve and the enclosing verticals and horizontal, are called **spandrels**; in grand arches these are often filled with sculptural reliefs.

There are many styles of arch which use this basic system. The simplest is the **round** or **stilted** arch. The **parabolic** arch describes a parabola, and the **horseshoe** arch a horseshoe. The **lancet** arch reaches in a curve to a sharp V point; the **ogee** arch does the same with two swirling curves; while the **trefoil** arch looks like a giant shamrock.

England's most famous arch, Marble Arch, dates from 1828.
It is built of white Carrara marble and is based on the
triumphal arch of Emperor Constantine in Rome. Fierce-
looking bearded heads occupy the quoins of each arch,
while the south-side spandrels contain languid female
Winged Victories carrying wreaths. On the north side,
reliefs depict three female figures representing England,
Scotland and Ireland (at that time part of the United
Kingdom). Its designer, John Nash, ran short of money
and other planned decorative sculptures ended up on the
façade of the National Gallery instead.

Marble Arch originally stood at the end of the Mall as
a grand gateway to Buckingham Palace, but was moved to
the northern end of Park Lane when the palace was
enlarged in 1851. Three years later it was used successfully
as a police base during a riot and its three internal rooms
remained as a small police station until the 1950s. Recently
there has been talk of moving it again, across the road
from its current position, where it is effectively marooned
on a traffic island, accessible only through a warren of
smelly underpasses. Despite a £75,000 facelift in 2004,
the Arch now serves only a decorative purpose.

  QUOIN

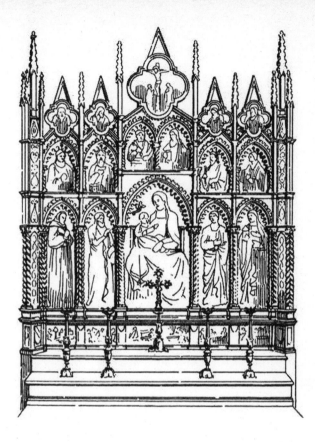

The Reredos

(pronounced reer-dos)

is the screen or decoration behind the altar
in a church. It may be painted or carved and
sometimes contains statues in niches. Alternatively,
it may be a tapestry or a simple drape.

There are other key parts of the sacred building which may
leave even churchgoers stumped for words. In a cross-
shaped church, the **transept** is the area set at right angles
to the main **nave**, which is the central section of the church

between the **west door** and the **chancel**, excluding the side aisles; this typically contains the **pews**.

The chancel is the area around the altar, often set up a step from the nave; this may end to the east in a polygonal, semicircular or vaulted space called the **apse**. In Roman Catholic and Orthodox churches, the chancel may also be called the **sanctuary**; and in some Protestant churches, the **presbytery**. This particularly holy part of the building may also be marked off with a rail or with a **rood-screen** (the word derives from the Anglo-Saxon *rode*, meaning a cross).

Medieval criminals and political offenders could claim 'the right of sanctuary' by taking refuge in a church, where they would be safe from the law. Sanctuary lasted for a fixed period of forty days, after which the criminal had to accept the charges against him and either face punishment or 'abjure the realm' and go into exile. However bad his crime, to lay hands on a criminal who had claimed this divine protection was an act of sacrilege, for which the punishment could be excommunication or a large fine (from a hundred shillings in a cathedral down to ten for a local chapel).

The Rowel

is the spiked revolving wheel at the end of a spur.

Rowels were a distinctive part of daily wear for cowboys in the wild west of America, both decorative, and useful when riding.

Six and a half centuries ago, they were an important part of a medieval knight's gear in battle, but also of the highest symbolic importance; indeed 'winning one's spurs' was regarded as acceptance into chivalric circles.

King Edward III (1312–77) was very keen on promoting chivalric behaviour. He set up a Round Table at his Windsor court, and had a rowel spur incorporated into his royal seal.

In 1348, Edward founded the Most Noble Order of the Knights of the Garter as 'a society, fellowship and college of knights'. The order began – supposedly – after an incident at a ball in northern France, when a garter slipped down the leg of the Countess of Salisbury as she was dancing. When the watching courtiers began to laugh at her, the King nobly stepped into the breach. Picking up her fallen garter he tied it round his own leg, saying: 'Honi soit qui mal y pense' ('Shame be to the person who thinks evil'). Subsequently the phrase became the motto of the Order.

Today, membership is limited to the sovereign, the Prince of Wales, and no more than twenty-four Companions. On ceremonial occasions, the Garter is worn around the left calf by knights, and around the left arm by ladies. On the death of a member, the badge and star and garter must be returned personally to the sovereign by the deceased member's nearest male relative.

The Samara

is the fruit of the ash, elm, sycamore or maple tree, in which the seed is encased in a double wing of light, papery plant tissue, which allows the wind to carry it some distance from its parent tree, often spiralling prettily as it goes. It's also colloquially known as a key, and some children call it a whirligig.

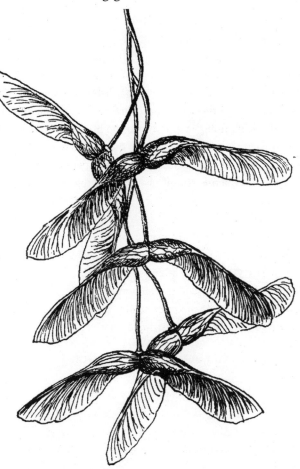

Maple samara

The *Shutter release*

is the correct name for the little flat button on
any camera – digi, Single Lens Reflex, point and
shoot, or even antique Box Brownie – which you
press to take a photograph.

Many of the other features of old-fashioned film cameras
are now the thingummies of yesteryear, remembered only
by photographers who spurn the convenience and

immediacy of the digital camera, and still talk lovingly of the **film rewind crank** (which wound the exposed film back into its cassette), the **take-up spool** (into which you inserted the pesky end of the new film) or the **pressure plate** (which held the film steady to receive the light in the right way).

Now digital cameras have swept the board. The good news for sentimentalists, however, is that many of the original names of camera parts persist, especially in the more expensive SLR digis. You still adjust the **aperture** or **f-stop ring** to let in more or less light through the lens. There is still a **shutter-speed control,** to set the time the **shutter** stays open – anything from one thousandth of a second upwards. There is still a **focus ring,** for manual focusing. On point and shoot cameras, you still have a **viewfinder,** as well as the more useful **liquid crystal display (LCD) screen.** Though most digis incorporate flash, swankier machines still have a **hot shoe,** the attachment for an external flash, which dates back to the days when there was no such thing as a built-in flash.

Digis also incorporate new features, such as a **control panel** to display camera settings. And instead of film they have **sensors,** the device which measures the intensity of light on each of its tiny pixels. And that thingummy which you can never locate when you need it, into which you put the camera to charge it up or download your pics, is of course the **cradle.**

Mr Dizzy Gillespie

A *Soul patch*

is a small patch of hair grown just below the centre of the lower lip. It may be either just a tuft or a strip all the way down the chin.

Soul patches have been around for centuries. Shakespeare had one, as did Vlad the Impaler. In the 1950s one was worn by trumpeter Dizzy Gillespie and earned itself the nickname 'the jazz dab'. It then became a fashion among beatniks, jazz, soul, and R&B musicians. Apart from looking cool, the patch provided a cushion of comfort when using a trumpet mouthpiece.

In the 1970s the patch was championed by such legendary hipsters as Frank Zappa, who wore a square one with a tailored handlebar moustache, and growling singer-songwriter Tom Waits. Temporarily in eclipse during the years of punk and the New Romantics, the patch returned triumphantly with grunge in the 1990s, now known as the 'flavour saver' and the 'cookie duster'.

Subsequently sported by such rebellious icons as Bruce Springsteen, Keanu Reeves and Fred Durst, the patch is clearly here to stay.

The *Sphygmomanometer*

is a reassuringly low-tech piece of kit with a very big name. It is simply a device for measuring blood pressure in the arteries.

It consists of a hand bulb pump, a unit that displays the blood-pressure reading, and an inflatable cuff that is wrapped around a person's upper arm, level with the heart, an inch above the elbow, over the brachial artery. A stethoscope is also used in conjunction with the sphygmomanometer to hear the blood-pressure sounds, which are called 'Korotkoff sounds' (after Dr Nikolai Korotkoff, a Russian physician who named them at the turn of the last century).

There are two numbers in a blood-pressure reading: **systolic** and **diastolic**. For example, a typical reading might

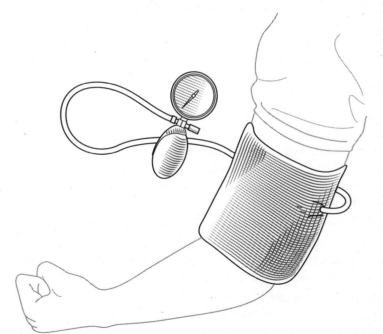

be 120/80. When the doctor puts the cuff around your arm and pumps it up, he is cutting off the blood flow. As the pressure in the cuff is released, blood starts flowing again, which the doctor can now hear in his stethoscope. The number at which the blood starts flowing, 120, is the measure of the maximum output pressure of the heart (systolic reading). The doctor continues releasing the pressure on the cuff, and listens until there is no sound. That number, 80, the diastolic reading, indicates the number when the heart is relaxed and pressure is lowest.

The Splat

is the flat piece of wood in the centre of a chair-back.

In the Middle Ages, when chairs first came into household use, such a piece of furniture was considered a very valuable item, and used only for high days and holidays.

At that time it was reserved for important visitors to the home, the seigneur, say, or the priest: they were offered what was often the only such piece of furniture in the house, and invited to be the 'chair man'.

Spogs

are the aniseed-flavoured jelly sweets in packets of Bassett's Liquorice Allsorts – and the only ones to contain no liquorice. They are coated with tiny pink or blue balls of sugary aniseed candy.

A story is told about the origin of the name Liquorice Allsorts. In 1899, sales rep Charlie Thompson dropped a tray of liquorice samples he was showing a client – mixing up every sweet he had. Fortunately, the client liked the way they now looked, and gave the salesman a big order. The name stuck, and the brand is still selling like hot cakes today.

Other sweets also have peculiar names. Boofuls, for example, is the name of the green, or lime, Jelly Baby; it's baby-talk for 'beautiful'. All the Jelly Babies, in fact, have names. The strawberry one is called Brilliant, the orange one is Bumper, Bubbles is the lemon one, Big Heart is the blackcurrant, and Baby Bonny the raspberry one.

When Jelly Babies were launched in 1918, to celebrate the end of the First World War, Bassett's called them 'Peace

Babies'. Shortage of raw materials stopped production during the Second World War, but it was resumed in 1953, when the sweets became known as Jelly Babies. Eight decades later, Cadbury Trebor Bassett – there were a few business mergers along the way – sell a billion Jelly Babies a year.

The Spoiler

is the hinged plate on an aircraft's wing which juts up as the plane touches down on the runway, acting as a brake, and bringing it within seconds to a (hopefully) graceful standstill. Fixed spoilers are also found on cars.

Spoilers work because they create an increase in **form drag** – the technical term for the slowing effect caused by an object as it travels through air. In this case the jutting-up spoilers have made the aircraft's form temporarily bigger, thus increasing its drag. (Car spoilers, by contrast, have the opposite purpose, to direct air away from the body and reduce drag.)

More important to the slow-down than form drag, however, is that the spoilers create a loss of lift, which means that the weight of the aircraft transfers from the wings to the undercarriage, making the brakes on the wheels more effective, and also reducing the chances of a skid.

The third crucial element of the aircraft's rapid stop is **reverse thrust**, when the jet engine directs its thrust towards the front rather than the back of the aircraft.

In flight, spoilers are used to help the aircraft either slow down or descend. Extended upwards to block the otherwise smooth flow of air over the surface of the wing, they create a **stall** over the section of the wing behind them, thereby reducing the **lift**, and allowing the aircraft to drop through the air without an increase in airspeed.

Not to be confused with the spoilers, usually just along from them on the **trailing edge** of the aircraft's wing, are the **ailerons**, another hinged control surface, the purpose of which is to control the **roll** of the aircraft around its longitudinal axis when turning or banking.

The correct use of spoilers is crucial. The following five aeronautical disasters were all at least in part owing to the misuse of spoilers:

✦ 5 July 1970. Air Canada Flight 621. The crew were on their final approach into Toronto airport on a clear, sunny day when the first officer mistakenly deployed the spoilers sixty feet above the runway. On the cockpit voice recorder he can be heard apologizing to the captain, just before the aircraft hit the runway hard, putting out an engine. Unaware of the damage, the crew took off again and reached 3,000 feet before crashing in a field eleven miles from the airport. All 109 on board died.

✦ 8 December 1972. United Airlines Flight 553. Approaching Chicago's Midway Airport, the pilot was instructed by the control tower to abort the landing and execute a 'missed approach' procedure. In the ensuing panic, the crew forgot to deactivate the spoilers. The plane stalled, before crashing into a row of bungalows one and a half miles north of the airport. Forty-five died, including two on the ground.

✦ 20 December 1995. American Airlines Flight 965. Approaching the Alfonso Bonilla Aragón International Airport in Cali, Colombia, the crew initially programmed the wrong destination into the Flight Management Computer. Subsequently their failure to deactivate the spoilers while climbing rapidly to avoid high ground led to the aircraft crashing into the side of a mountain at 8,900 feet. 159 died.

✦ 1 June 1999. American Airlines Flight 1420. The crew's forgetting to deploy the spoilers contributed to a runway overrun that left eleven dead and 110 injured at Little Rock National Airport, Arkansas. The plane crashed into a lighting pier, broke into three and caught fire.

✦ 17 July 2007. Tam Airlines Flight 3054. Owing to a deactivated thrust reverser, the pilots of this Airbus A320-233 were using the plane's spoilers on their own to brake at speed as they came in to Congonhas International Airport in São Paulo, Brazil. But the plane overran the runway, passed through a major highway, and crashed into a warehouse, where it caught fire. 199 died, including several on the ground.

The Sprocket

is the toothed metal wheel that meshes with a **chain** or **track** to transmit rotary motion between two **shafts**. It is an essential part of many machines, including tanks, film projectors and bicycles.

On a tank, the **drive sprocket** engages directly with the **caterpillar track**. In movie projectors, **sprocket wheels** engage with perforations (**perfs**) in the **film stock**. On a bicycle, sprockets of varying sizes engage a single chain to make up a system of **derailleur gears**. A typical ten-speed bicycle has two **driving sprockets** (at the front by the pedals) and five **driven sprockets** (on the rear wheel).

The derailleur is the mechanism that transfers the chain from sprocket to sprocket. It is usually operated by a **Bowden cable** attached to a **shift lever** on the handlebars.

The two-speed derailleur was invented in 1905 by the French cycling enthusiast Paul de Vivie. He was a wealthy young silk merchant who became hooked on cycling when a friend challenged him to ride his bicycle a hundred kilometres in under six hours. He subsequently gave up the silk business and opened a cycle shop, importing bicycles from Coventry, England, then the main centre of manufacture. He started a magazine called *Le Cycliste*, in which he wrote under the byline 'Vélocio'.

In 1889 de Vivie was riding his bicycle up a hill outside his home town of St Etienne, when one of his readers overtook him – smoking a pipe. De Vivie felt seriously challenged by this and devised a system whereby he had a gear that allowed him to go faster on the flat but at the same time cut him some slack on a slope. His solution was two chain rings, with – eventually, in 1905 – a derailleur to move the chain from one to the other. He called it Le Chemineau. Unfortunately for his heirs he failed to take out a patent for the derailleur, so made next to nothing out of this revolutionary system that transformed cycling for ever.

Despite the obvious advantages of the derailleur over the fixed gear, the mechanism didn't catch on immediately. De Vivie had to campaign for it in the pages of *Le Cycliste*, against opposition from the inventor of the Tour de France, Henri Desgrange, who wrote in *his* magazine, *L'Auto*, that variable gears were only for people over 45. 'We are getting soft,' he wrote. 'Come on, fellows. Let's say that the test was a fine demonstration – for our grandparents! As for me, give me a fixed gear!'

'After a long day on my bicycle,
I feel refreshed, cleansed, purified.
I feel that I have established contact
with my environment and that I am
at peace. On days like that I am
permeated with a profound
gratitude for my bicycle.'

Vélocio (Paul de Vivre)

The *Stifle*

is the joint in a horse's hind legs that corresponds to the human knee (though it's considerably higher up).

The inside and outside of the stifle have specific ligaments that keep the leg from bending excessively in either direction. These ligaments are called **collaterals** and can be torn or damaged if a horse stumbles or falls.

At the racecourse and elsewhere, jockeys, trainers and other equestrian professionals sometimes talk of a horse being 'stifled'. This describes a common problem, whereby the ligaments get 'locked' over the bony outcrop known as the **patella** (kneecap in humans). The horse will move differently, and in some cases may buck off its rider in an attempt to clear the problem.

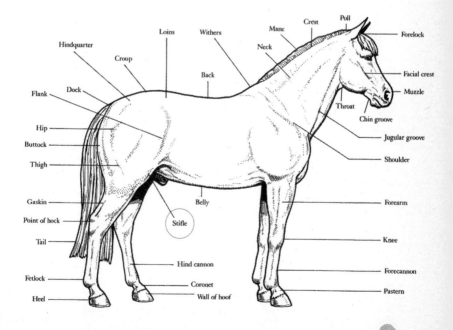

There are numerous other specialized names for a horse's body parts. The average punter may know **hoof, girth** and **tail,** and possibly **muzzle, withers** and **fetlock,** but will they know **poll, pastern** and **gaskin,** not to mention **crest, croup** and **dock?**

Horsey people are another group who can baffle you with their complex private language. Taking their animals round the school in **dressage** they know the difference between a **caracole** (half-turn movement) and a **piaffe** (very slow trot). At the racetrack, they speculate on the fortunes of a **maiden** (horse that's never won a race) or take their chances with a **nap** (most fancied horse). And that's before we've even got on to the names of all the tackle they actually put on their animals, from **snaffles** to **breeching tugs** . . .

The *Styptic pencil*

is a short stick (similar to a lipstick) of white anhydrous aluminium sulphate, which, by causing blood vessels to contract, is useful for staunching blood when applied to minor nicks or cuts – traditionally those caused by shaving accidents.

It's a particularly handy item for young men using razors for the first time. Indeed, the first-ever daub of styptic pencil – which leaves a stinging imprimatur for several minutes – is a painful rite of many a male adolescence.

The Tang

is the part of a knife blade that extends into the handle. The highest quality knives, as used by professional chefs, have the longest tangs, giving the knife ballast and balance.

The tang may be fitted into a slot in the handle, forming a **friction fit**, or held in place by **compression rivets**. When the knife has a **full tang**, running right the length of the handle, the two sides or **scales** of the handle are riveted to the tang on either side.

The **guard** – or **bolster** – is the barrier between the blade and the handle, which protects the hand, strengthens the knife and provides a counterbalance to the blade. The **heel** is the base of the knife, generally used for heavy cutting tasks. The **butt** or **neb** is the very end point of the handle.

Taupe

(pronounced tope)

is a warm, greyish-brown colour, commonly used for cars, leather sofas, computers, suede shoes and placemats among other essentials of modern life.

The word derives from the French name for the European mole *Talpa europaea*, and is described in some dictionaries as 'mole-brown'. But taupe has expanded over the years to encompass quite a range of colour possibilities, just so long as they have some element of greyish-brown or brownish-grey. Even professionals are not quite agreed as to what the colour strictly is, and colour charts boast varieties such as rose taupe, purple taupe, sandy taupe and medium taupe. In the late 1980s taupe was said to be the default colour for office supplies in the UK.

Many colours helpfully include in their names the three primaries – red, yellow and blue – or the simplest mixtures of the primaries – orange, green and purple. So there are going to be few prizes for guessing what a room painted in Tuscan Red might look like, or a dress that comes in Emerald Green. Other colour names offer a strong clue: apricot is clearly going to be a kind of orange, just as peacock is surely a blue. Others are too well known to surprise. Most people know that scarlet is a red, and emerald a green. But, like taupe, there are a few names that still baffle:

◆ **Écru** – the word comes from the French, and means cloth in its raw, unbleached, undyed state. It was originally a technical dye-house term and may describe silk, cotton, wool or linen. As such it is not strictly a colour. Until the start of the twentieth century, the term was enormously popular.

◆ **Eau-de-nil** – also from the French, meaning 'water of the Nile'; it describes a pale, yellowish-green colour.

◆ **Gamboge** – a transparent, dark mustard-yellow colour; this is a natural pigment, made from the yellow resinous gum of the Garcinia tree, found in south-east Asia. The word itself comes from the Latin for Cambodia, Gambogia.

◆ **Heliotrope** – a brilliant purple tint, supposedly a representation of the colour of the heliotrope flower. In Victorian times, it had a greyish element to it, and was one of the 'half-mourning' colours worn in the last stages of public grief.

◆ **Sien(n)a** – painters make much use of both raw and burnt sienna, which are respectively a yellowish ochre and a deep rich brown. They are both made from earth pigments. The textile colour Siena, however, which first appeared in 1874, is more of a deep reddish brown.

◆ **Verdigris** – once you realize this name also comes from the French, *vert-de-gris*, there might seem to be less of a puzzle about this colour. But *gris* here doesn't mean grey; the word derives from Old French *Verte-grez*, literally Greek green, so called because the pigment has been made from ancient times by corroding copper with wine-lees or vinegar. Verdigris forms naturally on copper surfaces exposed to moisture: the blue-green colour of all those weathered old domes you see in cities like Oxford and Copenhagen.

The Terminator

is the name for the line that divides the dark and the light parts of the moon.

It is clear and sharp, in contrast to the blurry line that divides light and dark on the Earth's surface as seen from Space. This is because the Earth has a 30-mile-high atmosphere, which scatters the light, while the moon has no air surrounding it. On the moon day becomes night in a few short minutes.

The moon spins in synchronous rotation to the Earth, meaning that it keeps almost exactly the same face turned to the Earth at all times. So humanity never got to see the **far side** of the moon until 1959, when it was first photographed by the Soviet probe *Luna 3*. The pictures surprised scientists by revealing a much barer surface than on the side of the moon we're used to seeing. The far side is not to be confused with the **dark side** of the moon, which is the hemisphere not illuminated by the sun at any given moment. When we look up at a new moon, we are in fact getting a full-on view of the dark side of the moon.

The moon is of a similar age to the Earth, 4.51 billion years old to the Earth's 4.55 billion years. But, unchanged by the development of the atmosphere and of Life, its surface retains a record of times when both globes were battered by debris left over from the formation of the planets. Three billion years ago, the Earthward face of the moon looked much as it does today.

As the moon **waxes** towards the first quarter, and then, **gibbous,*** towards a full moon, we get a clear view of its topography. The huge dark patches we can see are known

* When the illuminated part is greater than a semicircle and less than a circle.

as **seas** or *maria*, so called because astronomers once believed they were filled with water. They are in fact giant impact craters, formed when chunks of Space-matter crashed into the surface of the moon, carrying with them an energy equivalent to millions of hydrogen bombs. Mare Imbrium (the Sea of Showers), the crater whose main ring is some 1,140 kilometres wide, bears witness to a cosmic event which must have rivalled a thousand Armageddons. Later in the moon's life, these craters were filled with molten lava.

The history of the moon – that is, of our human understanding of it – involves many of the greatest names in science. In the sixth century BC, the Pythagoreans taught that the surface of the moon was like a mirror and the large 'spots' in the moon, visible to the naked eye, were reflections of the Earth's surface.

The Greek astronomers Hipparchus and Ptolemy, the Arabian Abu 'l Wafa', and the Dane Tycho Brahe all added to a growing body of moon observation over the next millennium or so. Leonardo da Vinci (1452–1519) made notebook sketches of the moon and first observed the variation in the 'spots'. A century later, the German Johannes Kepler (1571–1630) thought that the dark areas of the moon were land and the white areas water, and that the place might well be populated, by giants who would surely have to match in size these huge valleys, mountains and seas.

The invention of the telescope in 1608, by the Dutchman Hans Lippershey, changed the picture totally. Though the Englishman Thomas Harriot was the first to turn such an instrument to the night sky (in 1609), he was rapidly overtaken by the go-getting Italian professor of mathematics at Padua University, Galileo Galilei, whose

sketches and observations made through a more powerful telescope were rushed out in 1610 in a little book, *Sidereus Nuncius* (The Starry Messenger). He described the dark and light areas he saw on the surface of the moon as *maria* (seas) and *terra* (land).

The race was now on to produce a reliable map of the moon, which astronomers believed might solve one of the great scientific problems of that time, the search for an accurate measurement of longitude. In 1645 the Belgian Langrenus produced his *Philippian Full Moon*, a map adorned with proper names that he chose to honour the Catholic aristocracy of the time. This was quickly usurped by the efforts of a wealthy Polish brewer, Johannes Hevelius, who in 1647 published at his own expense the *Selenographia*, an altogether more lavish map of the moon. He imagined the moon as a distorted version of the classical world, complete with Mediterranean, Adriatic, Black and Caspian seas. Like Kepler before him, he took it for granted that our sister world was inhabited, coining the name 'Selenites' for the people of the moon.

But in this busy era of moon-mapping Hevelius's account was not to last long. It was replaced in 1651 by a map produced by a pair of Italian Jesuit priests called Grimaldi and Riccioli, who initiated the system of names for lunar landforms that still exists today. Their innovation was to name the features of the moon not after contemporary political figures, but after ancient and deceased philosophers, mathematicians and scientists – altogether less controversial and more enduring. In among these, naturally, were their own names, as well as a few of their Jesuit colleagues. Riccioli is also responsible for the poetic names of the moon's *maria*: the Oceanus Procellarum (the Ocean of Storms) and the Seas of Tranquillity, Fecundity and Serenity. The smaller dark patches on the moon he described as bays, lakes and marshes (including the Lake of Death, the Marsh of Sleep and the Bay of Rainbows). Riccioli's map was followed in 1680 by that of the distinguished French astronomer Cassini, but his names remain to this day.

TERMINATOR

A *Tessera*

is a small, square piece of material – ceramic, earthenware, glass, marble, mirror, stone or pottery – which when put together with other similar pieces creates a mosaic.

In the ancient world, tesserae were used for domestic interior decoration, generally for ornamenting floors and walls.

In Rome, a single tessera (often of wood or bone) would be stamped and used as a theatre ticket, or a pass for admission to a gladiatorial contest.

Tines

are the individual prongs on a fork.

In the cutlery triumvirate of knife, fork and spoon, the fork developed last. The knife came first, developed from implements of sharp-edged flint. By the Iron Age, knives were made of bronze and steel, with handles of wood, shell and horn. In Saxon England, a knife known as a *scramasax* would accompany its owner everywhere, to be used both for eating and as a defensive weapon. By the Middle Ages, food was eaten, in polite circles, with two knives, one holding the food while the other cut.

Forks were known to the Greeks and Romans, but were used mainly for cooking. It wasn't until the seventh century AD that the two-pronged fork made its way into the dining room, and then only in a sprinkling of royal courts in the Middle East. By the twelfth century the dining fork had reached Italy, and subsequently France. But even at the court of Charles V of France (1364–80), forks were used only for eating food likely to stain fingers. Subsequently, as late as the sixteenth century, they were thought to be an affectation, and people who dropped food while trying to use a fork for eating were ridiculed.

The fork didn't appear in England until the seventeenth century. A foodie's travel book by Thomas Coryate, *Crudities Hastily Gobbled Up in Five Months*, published in 1611, remarks with interest on the odd Italian custom of using a fork to hold meat.

The fashion must have caught on, because a few years later Ben Jonson was ridiculing those who used forks in his play *The Devil is an Ass*.

With the increasing use of forks, two tines gave way to a more useful three. By the early eighteenth century, in Germany, there were four-tined forks, which spread to England and were sometimes called 'split spoons'. By the end of the nineteenth century these were standard dining utensils. Five- or six-tined forks made a brief appearance but were subsequently rejected.

The fork appeared even later in America, where early colonists of refinement ate with knife and spoon. This led to the interesting difference in the way cutlery is handled in Britain and America.

In both places the knife is held in the right hand and the fork in the left. But in the US a single piece of food is cut with the knife, which is then laid down on the right edge of the plate, while the fork transfers to the right hand, and the food is speared or scooped with the fork tines-up. The fork is then transferred back to the left hand, the right hand picks up the knife again and the process repeats (described by American etiquette expert Emily Post as 'zigzagging').

In Europe, by contrast, the knife and fork are held continuously. The fork is generally tines-down throughout.

The Tip cup

is the part of an umbrella that sits just on top of the handle to stop water dripping down on to it. When the umbrella is closed, the **runner**, which pushes up the **canopy**, rests snugly against it.

An umbrella is a simple and beautifully designed object. Starting with the hook-shaped bit that we hold in our hands – the **crook handle** – we move vertically up the **tube** or **shaft**, passing the triangular **bottom spring**, which pushes in and springs back out to hold the runner in place when the umbrella is closed.

Just over halfway up the shaft is a part found only on telescopic umbrellas, the **centre ball spring**; this holds the upper part of the shaft in place when the umbrella is extended. Above that, holding up the runner and **stretchers** is the **top spring**, and above that, the **ribs**, which are connected to the stretchers with a **joiner**, a small jointed metal hinge. The canopy of the umbrella is sewn in individual **panels** to the ribs – a typical umbrella has eight. Centrally under the top of the cover is the **top notch**; immediately above that is the **open cap**, the end of the tube and finally the **ferrule**.

Among the qualities one might look for in a good umbrella are the comfort of the handle, the ease with which the umbrella is opened and closed, and the closeness with which the canopy segments are connected to the ribs.

The umbrella as we know it today is primarily a device to keep people dry in rain. But its original purpose was to shade someone from the sun (*umbra* is Latin for shade). About two thousand years ago, the sun-umbrella or **parasol** (literally, 'against the sun') was a common accessory for wealthy Greek and Roman women – men who used it

top spring

centre ball spring

bottom spring

tip cup

were subjected to ridicule, as it was considered a mark of effeminacy. It wasn't until the first century AD that Roman women took to oiling their paper sunshades, intentionally creating umbrellas for use in the rain.

Around this time the Chinese also used umbrellas, and indeed the Chinese character for an umbrella (*săn*) paints a picture of the object very clearly.

It remained a device for those of high rank; and in nearby Siam (Thailand), the king allowed only a chosen few of his subjects to use the umbrella.

But in the mid eighteenth century, in England, the travel writer and philanthropist Jonas Hanway set out to popularize the umbrella, carrying one with him on his walks around London (it became widely known as 'a Hanway'). The device was a threat to the coach-driving cabbies of the day, who were used to getting good fares on rainy days, so Hanway had to put up with a certain amount of mockery as he proceeded along the streets with his egregious accessory. (Made from cane or whalebone the eighteenth-century umbrella was not as light as later versions.)

One of the most important innovations to the umbrella came in the early 1850s when Samuel Fox conceived the idea of using U-shaped steel rods for the ribs and stretchers to make a lighter, stronger frame – the 'Paragon'. In the twentieth century, with cheap nylon replacing expensive silk, the umbrella became widely affordable.

A *Tittle*

If you've ever dotted an i, you have tittled, because the little dot above the i – and the j – is called a tittle.

Ever since the alphabet was invented, the dot above the i has been regarded as a measure of something very small indeed. In the Bible, Jesus is reported as saying (Matthew 5:18), 'For verily, I say unto you, till heaven and earth pass, one jot or one tittle shall in no wise pass from the law, till all be fulfilled.' In the Greek original of this gospel, the word rendered 'jot' is *iota*, the Greek name for the letter i – from which indeed jot derives.

The *Toast well*

is the correct name for the slot in a toaster into which you put the bread.

The mechanism that lifts the toast is, naturally enough, the **bread lifter**, and the bit at the bottom that collects the crumbs is the **crumb tray**. The wires inside that can endure the regular high heat needed to brown the toast are made of an alloy of nickel and chrome called **nichrome**.

In the early days of toasters, the browning of bread in such a machine was controlled by a mechanical clockwork timer; the only problem with this device being that the first piece of toast would be less well done than later ones, as the toaster had yet to warm up. So the perfect bit of toast might well be followed by the all too familiar sight of smoke rising from the machine – and burnt toast. Later toasters incorporated a **thermal sensor**, which allowed the first cycle to run slightly longer than later cycles.

Toasters come in all shapes and sizes: the two-slice, the four-slice, right up to the 'bachelor friendly' Sunpentown 3-in-1 Breakfastmaker, which combines a non-stick frying pan, a coffee-maker and a toaster all in one.

With the latest gadgets, toast can be more than just a taste sensation. The Breakfast-Art Image Toaster pops up bread decorated with a smiley face, a birthday cake, sunshine or a steaming coffee cup. But even that can't match the extraordinary CVC (constant volume combustion) toaster, which connects to a computer and allows you to print your own messages and pictures by blowing hot air through a gun on to the surface of your toast.

I never had a piece of toast
Particularly long and wide
But fell upon the sanded floor
And always on the buttered side.

James Payn, 1844

TOAST WELL

A *Toorie*

is the little bobble that sits on top of the round, brimless Scottish cap known as the **Balmoral**, or the alternative, wedge-shaped **Glengarry**, either of which may be worn as an accessory to Highland Dress. You will also find the toorie on the less formal bonnet called the **tam o'shanter**.

Other key parts of formal Highland Dress are of course the **kilt**, the traditional tartan skirt; the **sporran**, the round pouch that hangs in front of it, used to carry everything from wallet to car keys; the **Sgian Dubh** (pronounced *skeean doo*), the ceremonial dagger; and on the legs the **hose** (stockings), below which are found the tongue-less shoes called **Ghillie Brogues** or **ghillies**. Above all this is worn the **kilt jacket**. More elaborate ensembles may feature a **fly plaid**, a strip of pleated cloth thrown over the shoulder and fastened with a **plaid brooch**.

What is worn under the kilt remains a matter of mystery, not to mention amusement (at least to non-kilt-wearers). Not wearing anything is known as 'going regimental'. The origin of the term refers to the fact that Scottish regiments in the army are supposed to have worn their kilts in this way. Seasoned wearers advise that if this is your favourite style you are wise to sew a small flap of a less rough fabric in the groin section of the kilt.

When one kilt-wearing Scotsman encounters another he is allowed to ask whether his new acquaintance is indeed 'going regimental' by asking the question 'Are you a true Scotsman?' Needless to say, a true Scotsman wears nothing under the kilt.

Ullage

is the space in a wine bottle not occupied by wine.

If the top level of the wine is anywhere in the **neck** of the bottle that's regarded as a perfect **fill level** for a bottle of any age. Older bottles may have a lower level than this, owing to evaporation over time through the cork; for Bordeaux wines this is described in terms of the level's position on the **shoulder**, the rounded part at the top of the main bottle. **Top shoulder** is fine for any bottle older than fifteen years; **mid shoulder** is borderline, and may well indicate a wine that's not drinkable; **low shoulder** is unacceptable, except perhaps in the case of a very rare collector's item.

Burgundy and Pinot Noir are not measured in the same way as Bordeaux because the wine comes in bottles of a different shape, with a gently sloping upper half. Fill levels in such bottles are measured in centimetres – between cork and wine. Two centimetres or less is a good fill level for any wine; four centimetres is fine for a twenty-year-old bottle; six is too much, and again would only be countenanced if the wine is very rare and old.

Another interesting feature on most bottles of wine, which is guaranteed to stump all but the expert to name, is the **punt**, the hollow at the bottom of the bottle, also known as the **kick-up** or **dimple**.

There is no consensus on either the origin or the function of the punt. It serves perhaps to stop the bottle falling over; it increases the strength of the bottle; it makes the bottle look larger than it is; it's a useful place for the server of the wine to rest their thumb while pouring. These are just some of the explanations for the punt, all of which have some truth in them.

An *Umbel*

is a large flowerhead made up of a number of smaller flowers, each with an individual short stalk of roughly similar length which sprouts from a common centre. This lovely symmetrical formation is known to botanists as an **inflorescence** and the stalks are correctly called **pedicles**. The elderflower is an obvious example.

A number of vegetables are **umbelliferous**. The umbel seedheads of dill, coriander and fennel all make their way into the kitchen as useful herbs; carrots, parsnips and parsley too come from the same *Umbelliferae* family.

Another everyday umbellifer in British hedgerows is cow parsley, also known as wild chervil, Queen Anne's lace and keck. *Anthriscus sylvestris*, to give it its proper name, not only produces a large quantity of seed per growing season but also spreads rapidly through the horizontal stems known as **rhizomes**. Some consider it a weed. In the US, the state of Vermont has listed cow parsley on its Watch List of invasive species, and in Massachusetts and Washington sale of the plant is banned.

To make elderflower cordial, take 20 elderflower umbels, 1 lemon, 2 teaspoons of citric acid, 3½ pounds of sugar and 2½ pints of boiling water. Rinse the umbels thoroughly to remove dirt and insects, then put all the dry ingredients into a pan. Pour the boiling water over them and stir until all the sugar is dissolved. Skim off any surface scum, then cover with a lid or cloth. Stir twice a day for five days. Finally, strain all the liquid through muslin and bottle it.

The *Umlaut*

is the name for those two little dots you see floating over the letters of certain words, most of them German. It marks a change in the normal pronunciation of the letter.

In German, ä, ö and ü (alternatively spelled ae, oe, ue) describe different vowel sounds from a, o and u (sounds which have no direct equivalent in English).

In English and French, the same mark is used to indicate that two adjacent vowels should be pronounced as distinct sounds, as in Zoë, pronounced Zo-ee, not Zoh, and naïve. The two dots in this case are called a **diaeresis**.

The umlaut is one of a range of **accents** (or **diacritics**), which serve a similar function in a wide range of languages. In addition to the umlaut, the main accents are:

- Acute – as in émigré, José
- Grave – as in grandpère
- Circumflex – as in forêt
- Cedilla – as in soupçon
- Tilde – as in Señor
- Macron – as in rōmaji, kahakō
- Háček – as in Háček, Janáček

The generally agreed rules of contemporary English style are that you should use accents on the page only when they make an essential difference to pronunciation; but that if you use one, you should use all. They should be included in French, German, Spanish and Portuguese words and names, but left off all other foreign names. But if a foreign word is in italics, it should include its proper accents.

Although the English language rarely uses an umlaut, it is occasionally hijacked for marketing purposes. The umlaut in Häagen-Dazs ice cream is a case in point. It is a completely made-up name – the umlaut here is punctuational gibberish, but added perhaps to suggest an aura of olde-worlde European traditions and craftsmanship.

Some heavy metal bands have also favoured the addition of the bogus umlaut. Blue Öyster Cult (Don't Fear the Reaper) use one. And Mötley Crüe have two – but pointless excess in our musical heroes is *de rigueur* anyway.

Vibrissae

are the coarse hairs that grow around the mouths of most mammals. In humans they are found just inside the nostrils and serve to keep large particles from entering the nasal passages. In cats they are long and distinctive – and known as whiskers.

Vibrissae are generally thicker than other kinds of hair. They are circular in cross-section, and are the only hairs to taper all the way from the base to the tip. They contain no nerves, but are held at the base by a special follicle that is sealed in a blood capsule known as a **blood sinus**. If a vibrissa is touched, the blood amplifies the movement, and the resulting impulses are transmitted to the animal's brain, where they are a crucial source of information, particularly if other senses are limited by circumstances. Cats, for example, use their vibrissae to navigate and discriminate between surfaces in the dark. The vibrissae of seals are sensitive to vibrations from 50 to 1,000 Hz, and help the seals to detect prey in dark waters.

Clipping an animal's vibrissae takes away this acute sensory awareness. If you cut off a cat's right whiskers it will have trouble walking straight until they grow back fully. In tests on rats, the removal of vibrissae has been shown to affect not only their equilibrium and locomotion, but also their swimming ability, perception of depth and ability to discriminate between circumstances. In another study, cats deprived of vision from birth developed supernormal growth of their vibrissae.

Despite this, dogs of many breeds have their vibrissae clipped when on show in the ring; the whiskerless style is supposed to look cleaner.

Not all vibrissae are on the face: a squirrel has vibrissae on its ankles and some bats have vibrissae on the rump. Whales have no body hair remaining from earlier evolutionary stages except vibrissae.

A *Waldo*

is a mechanical hand-like device for manipulating objects by remote control. It's generally used in environments where it would be hazardous for humans to work.

The waldo is named after the main character in Robert A. Heinlein's novella Waldo (1942), which told the story of Waldo Farthingwaite-Jones, born such a weakling that he couldn't even hold a spoon. Refusing to allow this to hold him back, he developed a powerful mechanical hand, which he could operate remotely. With this and other inventions he became a wealthy man and built himself a home in Space.

The history of remote control is surprisingly long. The first patent for such a device was registered in America in 1893. Ten years later, the Telekino robot successfully executed commands by using electromagnetic waves; in 1906, its inventor Leonardo Torres Quevedo used it to guide a boat around the port of Bilbao in front of a huge crowd, which included the King of Spain.

The first remote specifically designed to control a television was developed by Zenith Radio Corporation in 1950. It was called the Lazy Bones and was connected to the television by a cumbersome wire, which careless users could sometimes trip over. Five years after that, Zenith developed a wireless remote called the Flashmatic. This worked by shining a beam of light on a photoelectric cell – the only problem with this being that the cell could also be activated by other light sources, so people found their television changing channel all by itself in bright sunshine, for example.

Six years later, the Zenith Space Command came out. This used ultrasound to change the channel and adjust volume. When the user pushed a button on the remote control, it struck a series of different bars, making clicking sounds of various frequencies which were picked up by circuits in the TV. The term 'clicker' began with this remote-control device.

When transistors were invented, electronic remotes were made that contained a crystal that was fed by an electric current oscillating at a high frequency. Unfortunately, the ultrasonic signal transmitted was within the frequencies audible to dogs, so pets could hear it and be disoriented by its use – as could some (younger, generally female) humans. Remotes today mostly use an infrared diode to emit a beam of light.

Despite their ubiquity, these useful aids to idleness remain without a more interesting name than remote control device (RCD). 'Chuck us the clicker, the doofah, the zapper, the thingummy,' we say, but to date nobody has come up with a better term for this crucial accessory to contemporary life. May we suggest the waldo?

Worsted

(pronounced wur-stid)

is a type of closely woven fabric made from long, combed staple wool. The word can also refer to the yarn itself, which may be used to make twilled fabrics like **whipcord, gabardine** and **serge**.

The name comes from the parish of Worstead in Norfolk. After the Norman Conquest of 1066 Flemish weavers began to migrate to England, attracted by the abundant supply of wool from Norfolk sheep (not to mention, perhaps, landscapes as flat as at home). Numbers increased during the reign of Edward III (1312–77)*, who was married to a Flemish princess, and encouraged weavers to come to England and 'exercise their mysteries in the

kingdom'. Weaving continued in the village – and in nearby North Walsham and Aylsham – until 1882, when the last surviving weaver of the area, John Cubitt, died aged 91. Hand-loom weaving had by that time been rendered redundant by the power-driven machines of West Yorkshire.

Worsted yarn woven with silk or cotton thread is known as **bombazine**.

* See **Rowel**, p. 171

The Xbox

is a video game console
produced by the Microsoft Corporation.

Besides the central square box, the console includes
one or more attached **controllers**, which feature all the
important thingummies that allow you to control the
action on the screen: two **analogue sticks** ('joysticks'), a
directional pad, two **analogue triggers**, and six 8-bit **digital
action buttons**, as well as back and start buttons. To be
even reasonably good as a player you must learn how to
manipulate all of these controls pretty much
simultaneously.

The Xbox was launched in 2001 to compete with two hugely
successful Japanese computer game machines – the Sony
PlayStation 2 and the Nintendo GameCube – at a time
when the video-game market seemed to threaten the PC
market which Microsoft had dominated so successfully
worldwide.

Initial demand wasn't strong, and in the UK the price
was dropped after one month from £299.99 to £199.99
(with early buyers being offered free games). The Xbox was
an unusually large console – so much so that it was known
in Japan as 'the coffee table'. A smaller model, the Xbox S,

launched initially in Japan, was released elsewhere in the world and gradually replaced the original bulky 'Duke'.

Of the launch games *Halo: Combat Evolved* proved a success with both critics and punters and by 2003 the Xbox had gained more sought-after games, such as *Tom Clancy's Splinter Cell* and LucasArts' *Star Wars: Knights of the Old Republic*. Subsequently, titles that had only been available on the PlayStation – such as the famous *Grand Theft Auto* series – were released in Xbox versions.

Further momentum for the Xbox came with the launch in November 2002 of the Xbox Live online gaming service, which allowed subscribers to play games online with others all around the world. By 2005, membership stood at two million. Whilst ultimately selling more units than the Nintendo GameCube, the Xbox finished a distant second to the all conquering PlayStation 2. Production of the Xbox was stopped in August 2005 and in November of that year the Xbox 360 was launched.

The Xbox 360 is a **seventh generation** video game console and competes directly with the Nintendo Wii and Sony's PlayStation 3. The main advantage of the Xbox 360 is its strong games catalogue and its ability to connect to Xbox Live; it can also play games and films in High Definition. The PlayStation 3 also has an internal hard drive and can play high-definition Blu-ray movies and games. The Nintendo Wii is the only one of the three not to have a hard drive; nor does it use High Definition. But it's cheaper than the other systems, and has a stylish controller, the Wii Remote, which looks like a TV remote and acts as a wireless pointing device. Due to this revolutionary controller and the inclusive, family nature of its games, the Wii is the runaway winner of the current generation of consoles. Eat, sleep and Wii!

The Yips

is half physical ailment, half psychological/ psychosomatic condition: the golfer's equivalent of the writer's block, the surgeon's shaky hand, the construction worker's dodgy back.

The ball is lying on the green. The golfer takes out his putter and bends over the ball, frequently squinting at the flag and back over to his ball, as he mentally calculates the line.

He's playing a foursome, and the other three keep a tremulous silence as he takes a practice putt, brushing the cut grass with the blade of his putter, before stepping up to the ball.

He stands over the ball – he knows what he has to do – but something, some cursed area in his brain won't let him putt; it is as if the club weighs a hundred tons, and the distance to the hole, well, he might as well be aiming a snowball at Jupiter. He can't putt today, as he hasn't been able to for nearly a year now; he just can't summon up the physical or mental control to perform the action . . . Tomorrow he may give up the game.

Such is the dreaded disease of golfers – the yips.

The Zarf

is the metal holder for a coffee cup (or glass) that has no handle.

The cardboard sheath in which a takeaway cup is carried can also be called a zarf, though it's often known as a **clutch**. Some people even use the word for the neoprene bottle-holders that are used to keep drinks cool in hot climates (known to Australians as **stubbie coolers**).

The word comes from the Arabic for container or envelope, as the device originated in the Middle East. From the thirteenth century AD, when coffee first became popular in the region,* the drink was served in handle-less cups made from glass or porcelain. These were then held in zarf – the plural is the same as the singular – made from copper, brass, silver and even gold, often heavily ornamented or set with precious stones. Zarf were also made from tortoiseshell, horn, ivory and wood.

* Coffee was first discovered in the ninth century, in the highlands of Ethiopia (still a major producer). From there, it spread up to Egypt and Northern Africa, then into the Middle East and on to Italy, from where it gradually reached the rest of Europe.

The *Zucchetto*

(pronounced zoo-ket-oh)

is the small skullcap worn by clergy members of the Roman Catholic Church.

The colour of the zucchetto (which means pumpkin in Italian), denotes the wearer's rank. Cardinals traditionally wear red ones, bishops and abbots wear violet, priests black. The big guy wears a white zucchetto.

Only bishops and cardinals may wear the cap during services. The cleric will start Mass wearing his cap, but must remove it at the commencement of the Canon – hanging it up on the short mushroom-shaped stand near the altar, called the **funghellino**. He may put it on again at the end of Mass.

Acknowledgements

Ian Cairns, Stan Criticos, Josh Dixey, Macy Egerton, Fredrik Elwing, Mike Farr, Glynis Fox, Carlo Giaquinto, Anthony Grayling, Lasse Gunnerud, Peter Hartley, Henry Holt, Rob Jenkins, Simon Jones, Rupert de Klee, Audrey Larman, Aedan MacGreevy, Tina Mackenzie, Keith Makepeace, Paul Manduca, Paige Mickel, Adrian Millsom, Alan Page, Gavin Pretor-Pinney, Guy Staight, GT, Norman Taylor, Carolyn Tolles, Gavin Weston, James Wilmot-Smith.

And, of course, Thayer and Jo.

Selected Sources

Architrave: see *A History of Classical Architecture*, Bruce Allsopp, Pitman, London, 1965; also *The Classical Orders of Architecture*, Robert Chitham, Elsevier/Architectural Press, 2005.

Besom: see *Quidditch Through the Ages*, Kennilworthy Whisp (J. K. Rowling), Bloomsbury/Whizz Hard Books, 2001.

Contrail: see *The Cloudspotter's Guide*, Gavin Pretor-Pinney, Sceptre, London, 2006; also *National Geographic News*, 14 June 2006 (nationalgeographic.com/news).

Cumulonimbus: see *The Cloudspotter's Guide*, Gavin Pretor-Pinney, Sceptre, London, 2006.

Desire Line: see Wildlife and Countryside, Public Rights of Way (www.defra.gov.uk).

Emoticon: see 'How an In-house Campaign Became a Global Icon', *Christian Science Monitor*, 4 October 2006; also 'Ad Executive Credited with Smiley Face', *New York Times*, 14 April 2001.

Garage: see *Last Night a DJ Saved My Life*, Frank Broughton and Bill Brewster, Headline, London, 2006; also *Popular Music Genres: an Introduction*, Stuart Borthwick and Ron May, Edinburgh University Press, 2004.

Gari: see *Sushi, Taste and Technique*, Kimiko Barber and Hiroko Takemura, Dorling Kindersley, 2002.

Grawlix: see *The Lexicon of Comicana*, Mort Walker, Museum of Cartoon Art, Port Chester, NY, 1980.

Niqaab: see *Arab Dress: a Short History*, Yedida Kalfon Stillman and Norman A. Stillman, Brill, Boston, 2000. Koran quote: Sura XXXIII: 59.

Payot: quote: King James Bible, Leviticus 19:27

Tines: see *The Evolution of Useful Things*, Henry Petroski, Alfred A. Knopf, New York, 1993.

Tip cup: see *Notes and Queries*, 8 June 1851.

Tittle: quote: King James Bible, Matthew 5:18

Umlaut: see *The Economist Style Guide*, Profile Books, London, 2005.

Worsted: see *History of Worstead* (www.worstead.co.uk).

Picture Credits